Six Principles for Building a Truly Inclusive School
A Call to Action for K–12 Leaders

Toni R. Barton, JD

Routledge
Taylor & Francis Group
NEW YORK AND LONDON

Designed cover image: © Toni R. Barton, JD

First published 2025
by Routledge
605 Third Avenue, New York, NY 10158

and by Routledge
4 Park Square, Milton Park, Abingdon, Oxon, OX14 4RN

Routledge is an imprint of the Taylor & Francis Group, an informa business

© 2025 Taylor & Francis

The right of Toni R. Barton, JD to be identified as author of this work has been asserted in accordance with sections 77 and 78 of the Copyright, Designs and Patents Act 1988.

All rights reserved. No part of this book may be reprinted or reproduced or utilised in any form or by any electronic, mechanical, or other means, now known or hereafter invented, including photocopying and recording, or in any information storage or retrieval system, without permission in writing from the publishers.

Trademark notice: Product or corporate names may be trademarks or registered trademarks, and are used only for identification and explanation without intent to infringe.

ISBN: 978-1-032-76224-1 (hbk)
ISBN: 978-1-032-75889-3 (pbk)
ISBN: 978-1-003-47764-8 (ebk)

DOI: 10.4324/9781003477648

Typeset in Palatino
by SPi Technologies India Pvt Ltd (Straive)

Six Principles for Building a Truly Inclusive School

This action-oriented guide details how school leaders can take an active role in transforming school systems so that they are truly inclusive—promoting belonging and academic success for exceptional learners and across all student subgroups. Centered around the key idea that learner variability is the norm rather than the exception, and that everyone from the school leader to the general education teacher to policymakers to community members must play a role, the book takes readers on a learning journey through student stories, self-reflection questions, goal-setting activities, practical tips, and community-based calls to action. It details six research-based core principles that provoke deep thinking and prompt actionable change, asking each reader to understand their role in disrupting the current status quo for exceptional learners. *Six Principles for Building a Truly Inclusive School* is key reading for school leaders, educators, and educational professionals learning how to be advocates and change makers for inclusivity in their schools and communities.

Toni R. Barton, JD, is a professor in the Education Leadership Program at Arizona State University and works with schools and organizations nationally, supporting them with designing systems and programs that improve outcomes for exceptional learners.

Other Eye on Education Books
Available from Routledge
(www.routledge.com/eyeoneducation)

Fostering Parent Engagement for Equitable and Successful Schools
A Leader's Guide to Supporting Families and Students
Patrick Darfler-Sweeney

Sparking Change to Promote Equity
Implementing Culturally Responsive Leadership Practices in Gifted and Advanced Programs
Javetta Jones Roberson and Kristina Henry Collins

Where Is the Teacher?
The 12 Shifts for Student-Centered Environments
Kyle Wagner

Relational Inclusivity in the Elementary Classroom
A Teacher's Guide to Supporting Student Friendships and Building Nurturing Communities
Christoforos Mamas, Shana R. Cohen, and Caren Holtzman

Improving Your School One Week at a Time
Building the Foundation for Professional Teaching and Learning, Second Edition
Jeffrey Zoul and Spiri Diamantis Howard

Contents

Meet the Author . . . . *vi*
Foreword . . . . *vii*
Acknowledgments . . . . *xi*
I'm Here Because I Had the Audacity . . . . *xiii*

Part 1 The Foundation 1

1 Introduction 3

2 The Problem: 20+ Years of Education Reform and Results for Who?! 14

3 Principle 1: Anti-Exclusionary Program Design 49

4 Principle 2: Inclusive Professional Learning 82

Part 2 The Big Three Systems 97

5 Principle 3: Person-First Culture 99

6 Principle 4: Student-Centered Instruction 137

7 Principle 5: Data Urgency 185

Part 3 Putting It All Together 203

8 Principle 6: Collective Responsibility 205

The Problem: Back Matter 213

Meet the Author

Toni R. Barton, JD, is a professor in the Education Leadership Program at Arizona State University and works with schools and organizations nationally, supporting them with designing systems and programs that improve outcomes for exceptional learners. She is the host of the podcast *School Disrupted* and has authored many articles on inclusive education. Her work has been mentioned in Forbes and she was named a national beacon in special education by the Center for Learner Equity. Toni founded the Inclusive Schools Leadership Institute at Relay Graduate School of Education, a national program that has supported leaders across more than 20 states and hundreds of school systems. She is a former principal and charter network director who started her career as a special education teacher in Washington, D.C. public schools. Toni holds a master of arts in teaching—special education, juris doctor, and bachelor of science in computer information systems. She is currently a PhD candidate at the University of Arizona.

Foreword

"I can see a lot of diversity stuff happening," Marianne, a junior at Terranceville High School, said. I had been invited to her school to facilitate focus groups as part of an equity assessment. Marianne was one of eight students who volunteered to participate in a focus group in which black students would be invited to share their experiences at the school. I had asked what sorts of equity and diversity initiatives they observed at Terranceville since school leadership instituted a five-year equity plan the previous year. "They've taped posters around the school," she continued. "We talked about bullying once in homeroom. At some point somebody hung flags all around the cafeteria."

Then she paused.

"It's weird," she said. "I can see that somebody is thinking about diversity. I can see a lot of diverse things happening here. But I can also say that it doesn't *feel* any different from how it felt before. Like, they can hang up all these posters, but I still see black kids getting in trouble for things white kids don't get in trouble for. Most teachers still have no idea how to respond when somebody says something racist." Several other focus group participants snapped in agreement.

Then Sondra, a Terranceville senior, said, "Yes, yes, yes. It makes you wonder who the diversity stuff is really for because it's not for us."

When I think about the conditions that undermine equity work in schools, I return repeatedly to the same observation. The primary problem when it comes to the persistence of educational inequity, bias, and injustice is not so much the scarcity of practical "DEI" strategies or of neat-sounding "belonging" initiatives. In virtually every school I've visited—hundreds of schools—I could look around and talk to a few people and find a long list of practical "DEI"-type things happening: festive celebrations of diversity, Black History Month assemblies, ceremonial displays of Safe Space stickers, efforts to make curricula a little less exclusive. But when I talk with students or staff who bear the brunt of the inequity, bias, and injustice, one of their most common concerns is that these practical, high-optics expressions of institutional inclusion never quite manage to change their experiences at their schools. The trouble is, there is nothing about celebrations or assemblies that identify and eliminate ableism, racism, heterosexism, or any other form of injustice. If we're not careful, these kinds of initiatives can become high-optics, low-impact stand-ins for equity and justice; they can, and in many schools *do*, become cover for adults who want to appear committed to equity and inclusion—who may even see themselves as equity champions—but who do not have the will to do what it takes to eliminate inequity.

What do you see when you take a deep, truly inquisitive look at the diversity and inclusion efforts at your school? Are they transformative? Do they identify and eliminate inequity? Is it all baby steps and tiptoeing? What do they change fundamentally about how your school operates? Who are the diversity and inclusion efforts for? What would the Mariannes and Sondras in your school have to say about them?

This, I'm afraid, is the conversation we have too infrequently in education. It's easy to assume that the biggest barrier to equity progress is blowback from the people who most explicitly resist that progress. It's easy to blame the equity poo-poohers. But if we're going to be totally honest, we have to wonder whether a bigger barrier might be the tendency even among many supposed equity champions toward those high-optics, low-impact equity approaches.

This is the tendency my super-genius colleague Katy Swalwell and I hoped to push against when we created the equity literacy framework. Many educational leaders and changemakers have drawn on equity literacy in their efforts to imagine a transformative approach to equity. In most cases, the results have reflected a watered-down version of equity literacy, reshaping it as personal awareness while understating its systemic nature. My first hint that I was in for a transformative ride reading this book was seeing Toni Barton foregrounded the most transformative elements and values of equity literacy as she mapped out a powerful, unique, systemic framework for justice-based educational transformation.

What most inspired me about this book is that Barton wasted no time or page space. This book starts where most conversations about disability justice in schools—or, really, any form of justice in schools—never quite seem to arrive. We're urged to think and act institutionally and systemically, not just interpersonally. Sure, the book nudges us to reflect on our own biases and presumptions, but Barton clarifies that the inward work does not magically produce institutional change. She refuses to accept that individual educators ought to take on the burden of transforming systemic breakdowns. She rejects savior-laced deficit views that unfortunately are prominent in discussions about disability and inclusion. She provides big, broad context, but doesn't leave us flailing in the bigness. Instead, she provides us with the knowledge and tools we need to create change within our spheres of influence. And she brings a powerful intersectional view, never hiding racism or other forms of oppression behind ableism.

If you're looking for *ten easy steps to make a school a little less inequitable without having to confront my harmful ideologies*, this is not the book for you. No, actually, this *is* the book for you. Please read it.

As a reader and a learner, what I most appreciate about this book, though, is that it is based on principles and commitments, on values and reimaginations, not on those detached kinds of "DEI" strategies that dominate equity initiatives in schools. The principles pushed me toward the kind of root cause analysis and problem-solving that is crucial when it comes to educational equity and justice. Sure, Barton steps us through key practices for operationalizing these principles, but only after she has stepped us toward deep, transformative understanding. She understands that the practical stuff is driven by values. If we adopt the wrong values, the practical stuff is bound to do harm or to focus on fixing problems that don't exist, exacerbating injustice. We spend way too much time and far too many resources in education trying to solve problems that don't exist, like supposed resilience shortages in black and brown communities.

I'm cautious about framing this book as predominately values-based because I worry some educational leaders or other potential readers might read this perspective and think, *well, then, this book doesn't sound like it has much practical value.* That's the pesky obsession with practicality. It is, in my view, a substantial part of the mess we're in. So let me clarify my bigger point: the principles in this book and the values underlying the principles are, in the end, far more practical than the disconnected, decontextualized practical strategies that fill too many books about education because they provide guidance for every practical decision, we, as educators, might make about ableism and inclusion and, really, about any equity and justice issue. As I often argue, in the end, the ideological is practical because practice is informed by ideology.

That, in essence, is what Toni Barton gifted me—gifted all educators—in this book. She shifted the ways I think about and, as a result, the ways I will act on inequity in schools and beyond. Shift a perspective, transform every related practice.

—Paul C. Gorski, founder of the Equity Literacy
Institute and coauthor (with Katy Swalwell)
of *Fix Injustice, Not Kids and Other Principles
for Transformative Equity Leadership*

Acknowledgments

This book would not have been possible without the wise counsel of my beloved mentors, colleagues, and peers. I want to begin with a special thank you to Paul Gorski for his support and contribution to this work. You have had an invaluable influence on the field and my own work. I am grateful for your partnership in this effort.

To Zaretta Hammond, honored is an understatement. I can't thank you enough for your wise counsel and feedback on Chapter 5. Your guidance strengthened this chapter, and I know it will push the practice of everyone who reads it. The impact you have had on our profession is an inspiration, and I hope your contributions to this book push my readers at least half as much as your work has pushed our field.

Katie Novak, your accolades about my vision for this book mean more than you know, and I thank you for taking the time to read my first chapter. You have been someone whose work I've admired for many, many years, and it is an honor to have your acknowledgment of my efforts.

Megan Ohlssen and JT Schiltz, thank you for your nuggets of wisdom from our many great conversations that show up throughout this book. I am grateful for how you pushed my thinking and your impact on my work.

Megan Sands, thank you for your copyediting obsession. Your feedback on this book and partnership over the years has been invaluable!

MaryAnn, you were my first mentor as a teacher, and I am grateful for the full-circle opportunity for you to provide feedback on my first book. Thank you!

To the leaders who allowed me to share your stories as a learning tool for the readers of this book, I hope your work inspires them as much as it has inspired me.

To all of my former students, your journeys inspire me to strive to be better every single day. My work is done in honor of your tenacity, your perseverance, and your struggles. I hope that the next generation of students benefits from the wisdom I am able to share because of you.

Darryl and Isaiah, this book is for you. Your journeys as students are what inspired me to become a teacher and a principal working tirelessly to become an unapologetic advocate for students who deserve to belong in schools where educators have the knowledge and willingness to effectively support them. Without you, this book would not exist. I love you forever.

I'm Here Because I Had the Audacity

Picture this: A bright young first grader named Darryl, full of curiosity and potential. One day his teacher made a call to his mom that would change everything. "I have concerns about Darryl that I'd like to talk to you about," she continued, "I'm concerned about his fidgety behavior being disruptive to others, and I suggest he be evaluated for special education services." Shock and concern rang through Darryl's mom's entire being. I am Darryl's mom.

Completely surprised, I immediately thought to myself, "How could it be that her concerns outweighed my son's strengths to the degree that he needed to be in special education? He's reading chapter books, making friends, and loves school." Being a recent law school graduate, I had no expertise or understanding of special education, but what I did know was that I needed to learn more. Determined to make an informed decision about whether to have him evaluated, I dove into the world of special education and how it affects black boys like my son. What I discovered shook me to my core.

I will not allow my son to become a statistic! I learned that our educational system has historically struggled when it

> "Your son needs to be in special education because he's fidgety."

comes to special education, especially as it relates to black boys and special education. When it comes to kids like my son, the system is crippled by biases, stereotypes, and exclusionary mindsets and practices, leaving kids like him feeling out of place, without access to high-quality instruction, and in many cases, unsuccessful in school. I refused to let this be Darryl's story. Instead, I sought a new path—a different neighborhood and a different school that celebrated differences and nurtured potential where teachers didn't jump to conclusions. That decision changed everything; Darryl found himself in a supportive, diverse environment where he thrived, free from the labels that once threatened to completely change his life trajectory.

What if that teacher knew that 16 years later, Darryl was destined to graduate from Pennsylvania State University with a degree in biobehavioral health and teach middle school science at the school I was once the principal of? Would she have still referred him to special education? If he had ended up in special education, would he have become a college graduate? This experience lit a fire within me because I knew Darryl's path would have been different had I not had the audacity to challenge his teacher's inclination to label him and make him someone else's responsibility simply because her classroom was not designed to work for him.

There are countless students who end up in special education because traditional classroom design does not meet their needs. Parents should not have to move to a new town or change schools because of a mismatch between the school and the learning needs of their child.

You're going to be appalled! My son's experience led me to abandon my law degree for a career in education, and I became a special education teacher in Washington, D.C. I realized immediately that what my research unearthed was true, being in special education was not likely to lead to positive outcomes for certain student groups, and there were serious flaws in the design of school and special education. Many alarming things happened during my early teaching career, too many to name, but I will highlight a few that still shock me to this day.

In my first year, I was assigned to a self-contained classroom of students with emotional disabilities whose needs were so significant that they were placed in a specialized program. After joining an alternative certification program, I was assigned to this classroom with only two months of summer training.

- ♦ That classroom had students across grade levels and the principal gave me the teacher's guides for all subjects and all grade levels and expected me to teach all of them.

- I had many students who did not know how to read, and I had never heard of the science of reading, had no reading intervention materials, and my students were not pulled out of class for interventions of any type.

> Despite our best intentions, a critical mass of students is being harmed by school.

- In my third year, I left the district school for a charter school with an inclusive model.

Two of my students followed me, and within two years, one of them left special education completely, and the other had his classification changed from Emotional Disturbance to Specific Learning Disability in Math. This is where I first realized the power of a learning environment.

I knew instantly that school leadership and teacher preparation would be my path because I did not want any other teachers to have the experience that I had.

I chose to become an expert! My first leadership role was as a special education director, where I mastered the skill of advocacy, strengthened my understanding of learner variability, and learned to prioritize students over the system. Next up, I would build my instructional chops during my tenure as an academic director and principal, where I spearheaded a Response to Intervention and Positive Behavior Support Initiative leading over 70% of our students to attain rigorous growth goals within one year—in a school were over 50% of the students had special education plans. We revamped the schedule across all grades, K–8, added a mandatory intervention and enrichment block for all students, trained all teachers in the science of reading and effective reading intervention, implemented an evidence-based reading and math curriculum, implemented and built teacher capacity in positive behavior supports, and collected and strategically responded to student data. I took this experience and growing knowledge base to a new network of schools where I turned around one of the lowest performing schools in the city, now a Blue Ribbon school, under the tutelage of my then assistant principal. She took over the principal role as I transitioned into a network leadership role, coaching leaders across six schools. Those combined experiences prepared me for my next role, designing and leading the Inclusive Schools Leadership Institute, where I trained hundreds of leaders across the United States on the characteristics of inclusive data, culture, and instructional systems designed to meet the needs of learners with diverse needs.

The design of the system must change! Fast-forward, after spending 20 years in education, I have learned that system design flaws are ingrained in the DNA of our education system. Consequently, despite our best intentions, a critical mass of students is being harmed by school even as you read this sentence. I have spent the last 20 years committed to figuring out and learning what works for kids like Darryl and my former students. What worked for the kiddos in my first inclusive classroom was high expectations, access to grade-level content, varied peer models, intensive intervention, targeted small-group instruction, and a positive, caring environment. Those practices are core to the principles outlined in this book.

Do you have the audacity? My goal is that this book is a catalyst for change as I call on parents, teachers, and leaders to have the audacity to challenge the status quo, dismantle barriers, and help create schools where no student's potential goes untapped, and every child flourishes. Making this a reality will require leaders to intentionally design school to meet the diverse needs of their students. This will take proactively seeking to build your understanding of how to create inclusive school environments, a willingness to question whether existing policies and practices are promoting or preventing student success, and actively working to remove barriers to success for every student in support of, not in spite of, their differences.

I hope that the stories and knowledge shared in this book inspire you to be a leader who is determined to make school work so that every student and parent feels welcomed, supported, and successful because of your leadership.

I can't wait to hear how it goes!

Part 1
The Foundation

1

Introduction

Introduction

If you are reading this book, you believe that schools should be inclusive and effective for all learners, regardless of their abilities or disabilities, and you are committed to learning how to make that happen. At the heart of this book is a set of beliefs that can serve as a guide for leaders striving to create transformative and inclusive environments.

All students deserve to be successful in school regardless of ability or identity marker.

Schools should be designed to support learners across the spectrum of variability.

- ♦ Students across the spectrum of variability deserve to learn from and alongside one another.
- ♦ Individual differences should be recognized and celebrated.

♦ Educators should be empowered with the skills and knowledge needed to support learners across the spectrum of ability.

You likely know that despite over 20 years of school reform efforts such as—*No Child Left Behind, Race to the Top, and Every Student Succeeds Act*—effective, inclusive schools continue to elude leaders, and students who need school the most have either failed to make progress or are falling further behind (see Table 1.1).

> *Reflect:* Review Table 1.1. Have any subgroups in grades 4, 8, or 12 made meaningful progress in the past 20 years? What does this make you wonder?

Furthermore, concerns about the lasting impacts of the COVID-19 pandemic and the growing demands of today's "TikTok generation" demand a new approach to school. These concerns include the following:

♦ Greater variation in academic performance within classrooms, making it increasingly challenging for teachers to address all students' needs.
♦ Rising behavioral and mental health needs among students.
♦ Difficulty in effectively supporting students with learning and behavioral needs.

These challenges illuminate an urgent need to empower educators with the tools and resources needed to create classrooms that are responsive to students' varying needs. Transforming schools with inclusive education at the foundation can be a solution. If we reframe neurodiversity as the norm by embracing the idea that all learners possess unique variations in their abilities and design comprehensive systems that accommodate the full spectrum of learner variability, we can support the varying needs in our schools.

TABLE 1.1 National Assessment of Education Progress. Twenty-Year Performance Analysis of Achievement Gap Between Subgroups and General Education Students

Subgroup	Reading Gap						Math Gap					
	2003			2022			2003			2022		
Grade levels	Grade 4	Grade 8	Grade 12	Grade 4	Grade 8	Grade 12	Grade 4	Grade 8	Grade 12	Grade 4	Grade 8	Grade 12
Student with a disability	−35	−41	−45*	−40	−36	−39*	−22	−39	−39*	−28	−36	−35*
English learner	−33	−41	−39*	−31	−38	−52*	−22	−37	−30*	−23	−36	−42*
Eligible for National School Lunch Program (NSLP)	−28	−25	*	−28	−23	*	−23	−23	*	−26	−27	*

Key:
* Grade 12 Data.
◆ Students with disabilities reflect the years 2005 compared to 2019.
◆ Eligible for NSLP data is not available.

Introduction ◆ 5

There are several harsh truths that make the case for the principles outlined in this book:

- **Schools are comfortable failing certain students.** Because we are maintaining a status quo of "failure" for certain student groups in school, we need to define and disrupt the status quo.
- **Schools see disability and learner variability as abnormal.** We need to shift our perspective on disability and neurodiversity.
- **There is no "average" learner.** Schools are designed for the so-called average learner. Academic and behavior systems do not support learner variability and need to evolve.
- **Everyone isn't pulling their weight.** Collective responsibility for supporting students with learning or behavioral needs is not the norm. All educators must be expected to have the skills to support learner variability in their classrooms.

Shifting this paradigm will require confronting traditional perspectives and structures and embracing change. It will require truth-telling about how certain students are being harmed by school, increased accountability for the dismal academic performance of subgroups, and a commitment to moving from traditional reform efforts to a focus on transformation.

The Opportunity

Throughout my career, I have served in many different roles, gaining a broad perspective and significant expertise. I served on a national working group on inclusive leadership, designed a national training program for school-based and systems-level leaders, trained hundreds of educators across the country, and served in various school leadership roles, including school principal. Educators are hungry for progress, systems are flawed, and change is hard.

As a result of those experiences, I have drawn one major conclusion: **there is no equity for exceptional learners without disruption**—disruption of prevailing belief systems, disruption of common practices, and disruption of existing systems. The goal of this book is to catalyze our field toward radical action.

My goals are to

- provoke you to take action,
- build your orientation toward inclusion and expertise in inclusive practices,
- outline practical guidance for improving outcomes for diverse learners, and
- provide opportunities and tools to support action planning.

You will examine six actionable principles, grounded in research and practice, for building truly inclusive schools. Each principle is supported by a compelling call to action designed to challenge your thinking and compel you to transform traditional thinking and systems to better meet the needs of the range of learners in your school.

This will be hard. Change toward inclusive education requires technical and social transformation. Such transformation involves careful consideration of the underlying structures and dynamics of existing systems and evolving those systems (Taylor & Sailor, 2023). This is why, in many cases, trying to bring about significant change ends with systems reverting to their original state (2023). It is much easier to tinker around the edges and implement bite-sized improvements, but that is no longer sufficient. We can't continue to fail students because change is hard and messy. No matter what, it will be hard and messy, so I challenge you to lean into the mess. Your student's lives depend on it (Table 1.2).

The Six Principles

TABLE 1.2 The Six Principles of a Truly Inclusive School

Principle	Call to Action	Description
Anti-Exclusionary Program Design	Design for marginalized learners.	Academic, behavior, and data policies, practices, and protocols are grounded in inclusive values and purposefully designed to promote growth for students across the spectrum of ability.
Inclusive Professional Learning	Empower all educators to understand learner variability.	Professional learning activities designed to empower all educators to create inclusive learning environments that promote belonging and academic success for all learners.
Person-First Culture	Reframe discipline systems as social-emotional support systems.	An approach to behavior and discipline that promotes a welcoming and affirming environment designed to foster safety, belonging, and well-being.
Student-Centered Instruction	Disrupt general education so all kids can learn.	An academic approach designed to drive growth for all learners by prioritizing and intensely supporting the individual needs, strengths, and differences of each student.
Data Urgency	Collect data frequently and respond immediately.	Emphasizes the immediate and consistent collection of data to allow educators to respond swiftly to student needs.
Collective Responsibility	Commit to being a part of the solution, no matter your role.	Educators must break down silos and take joint responsibility for the growth of all learners.

Book Structure

Part 1: The Foundation

Part 1 establishes the need for this book, outlining the current practices, systems, and mindsets that are supporting the lack of progress in school for exceptional learners—students with disabilities, multilingual learners, and other diverse learners. In this section, you will define the status quo that exists in your own context, setting the foundation for your action planning over the course of this book.

- **Chapter 1** – *Introduction*
- **Chapter 2** – *The Problem*: 20+ Years of Education Reform and Results for Who?!
- **Chapter 3** – *Principle 1*: Anti-Exclusionary Program Design

Part 2: The Big Three Systems

Part 2 outlines the core practices for improving culture, instructional, and data systems to improve outcomes for the range of learners in a school. Here you will examine how to design systems that support learner variability in schools, reflect on the presence of these practices in your own context, and set targeted goals.

Leaders will not be able to effectively implement new practices or policies in data, culture, or instruction without appropriately considering the elements of change management. Each chapter in this section ends with a set of considerations to support the change management process for each school-wide system.

- **Chapter 4** – *Principle 2*: Inclusive Professional Learning
- **Chapter 5** – *Principle 3*: Person-First Culture
- **Chapter 6** – *Principle 4*: Student-Centered Instruction
- **Chapter 7** – *Principle 5*: Data Urgency

Part 3: Putting It All Together

There are various stakeholders who impact the ability for students to be successful in school. Each of those stakeholders can play a role in improving the experience of exceptional learners, and the chapter in Part 3 outlines concrete next steps to help play a more meaningful role. This section summarizes concrete and achievable strategies and solutions for collaborators: educators, families, system-level leaders, funders, and policymakers who are essential partners in creating inclusive systems that prioritize students' diverse needs.

- **Chapter 8** – *Principle 6*: Collective Responsibility

Your Role

The book's content provides specific benefits to anyone who cares about ensuring school works for all kids. Acknowledging that each reader has a unique perspective and role in promoting inclusive education practices, the following are specific objectives based on your role. Keep these goals in mind as you dive in.

For Leaders
- Challenge and expand existing mindsets to drive transformative change through inclusive education practices.
- Examine the characteristics of culture and behavior systems that support learner variability and promote belonging.
- Examine how to transform grade-level instruction to support the range of needs in a classroom.

For Families
- Deepen your understanding of inclusive education practices and their potential impact on your child's education.
- Challenge and examine your own beliefs about disability and inclusion.
- Understand your role and responsibility in promoting inclusive education.

For Policymakers
- Gain insights into best practices essential for inclusive schools and assess the alignment of current policies with inclusive education practices and identify opportunities to innovate.
- Understand the importance of championing systemic change and pushing beyond incremental progress.

For Education Support Organizations
- Gain insights into best practices essential for inclusive schools and assess the alignment of your current programming and practices with inclusive education practices and identify opportunities to innovate.

- Gain insights into how to support transformative change within the schools you support.
- Build an orientation toward inclusive thinking to push beyond perceived and existing limitations to partner with schools to create inclusive environments.

YOUR ROLE

Reflect: Answer <u>one</u> of the questions below.
1. *Choose your lens and highlight one benefit that seems most interesting to you or is aligned with your individual priorities.*
2. *What is one thing you hope to gain from reading this book?*

Chapter Elements

To support goal setting and action planning, each chapter includes a common structure and set of elements to support readers:

- **Student Story**: Each chapter begins with a student story designed to provoke your thinking around each topic.
- **Provoking Questions**: Change happens when you are challenged. With that in mind, each chapter will begin with a question designed to provoke you to reflect on true notions of equity and whether what is currently happening in your context is driving toward true equity.
- **Pro-Tips**: Each story is followed by an aligned pro-tip outlining the shift in thinking required by each principle.
- **Inclusive Habits**: A list of positive behaviors or routines that contribute to achieving the goals outlined in the chapter.
- **Targeted Reflections**: Each chapter includes targeted questions to promote learning and support action planning.
- **Action Planning Prompts**: A goal setting template for setting targeted goals aligned to your key learnings.

FIGURE 1.1 QR Code for Digital Resource Access. This QR code provided direct access to supplementary digital resources supporting the content discussed in this section.

- **Parent and Stakeholder Tips**: Each principle can be applied to all stakeholders who play a role in a student's academic journey. Each chapter outlines potential next steps that parents and other stakeholders (e.g., policymakers, philanthropists, education support partners) can apply in their context.
- **Note-Taking Tool**: Use the QR code (Figure 1.1) to download the advanced organizer, which will support your engagement in this text. Use the tool to capture notes and key ideas as you read.

An Integrated Framework for Equity

This book is grounded in the Blueprint for Inclusive School-Wide Schools© (hereinafter the BLISS Framework), a research and evidence-based framework that outlines the elements of an effective inclusive school. This tool originated from the Inclusive Culture Inventory, a tool I designed to support leaders in Relay Graduate School of Education's Inclusive Schools Leadership Institute. It has been used to build the expertise of hundreds of leaders across every region in the United States.

Leaders are often peppered with and fatigued by shiny new initiatives and programs. This book is not that! This framework is the first K–12 leadership framework that intentionally integrates the leading equity frameworks into one concrete tool that is more than just a rubric or a checklist. This framework outlines a set of artfully crafted principles that will help you design school-wide systems in an intentional and strategic way so that school truly works for *every* learner. The framework itself is included in the "Appendix" of this book.

My hope is that after diving into this book through deep reflection and action planning, you will be able to shift from attempting to implement separate and disconnected equity initiatives to intentionally eradicating ableist systems in your school.

Bibliography

Taylor, J. L., & Sailor, W. (2023). A case for systems change in special education. *Remedial and Special Education*, 45(2), 125–135. https://doi.org/07419325231181385

2

The Problem

20+ Years of Education Reform and Results for Who?!

In This Section

> **CHAPTER CONTENTS**
>
> ♦ Will You Answer the Call to Action?
> ♦ The Status Quo Is Troubling
> ♦ *Problem 1*: The Knowledge Deficit
> ♦ *Problem 2*: The Ownership Challenge
> ♦ *Problem 3*: The Design Flaw
> ♦ What Is the Root of the Problem?

This chapter outlines the problem at the heart of this book, *certain students are being chronically failed by school*—students with disabilities, neurodivergent learners, English language learners, and other historically marginalized groups. I'm calling on you to answer the call to disrupt the existing status quo and move toward *truly* inclusive schools! If you are ready to dive into this challenge, this is the book for you, but if you are looking for a magic bullet or a list of shiny new practices, you have come to the wrong place. You could have picked up one of many other books on inclusive education that outlines what works. We know what works. Most of these books articulate the same set of practices. The problem is there is a gap between knowing and doing. To address this, our work together will be twofold. First, we will build a common understanding of six principles that can guide leaders toward designing inclusive school-wide systems. Second, we will answer, "Why do we *know* what to do but don't see consistent evidence of it across our schools?"

This book has three goals, to inform, provoke, and compel. It will **inform** you by building or strengthening your expertise in *effective* inclusive practices. It will **provoke** you by challenging conventional norms, beliefs, and practices related to inclusive education *and* **compel** you to act by asking you to identify concrete next steps. Your work starts now. Reflect honestly, leaning into the hard questions is necessary to move the needle for your students.

Reflect on the following:

1. Are your most vulnerable students benefiting from school?
2. Are you okay with the chronic failure of students with disabilities and other marginalized learners?
3. How are your policies, practices, and protocols contributing to the problem?
4. Is general education flawed?

Will You Answer the Call to Action?

Schools should be places where students feel welcomed, respected, and connected to their community. They should be places where adults hold shared accountability for ensuring the academic, social, and emotional needs are met for *all* students, not just the easy ones. Most importantly, schools should be *truly* inclusive, meaning they promote belonging and academic success for all students, regardless of ability or difference. Building truly inclusive schools calls for leaders who are willing to set a vision for inclusivity, align academic and behavior systems to that vision, and measure their success by whether they are living up to that commitment.

Are you willing to be that leader?

Welcome to the journey!

For as long as I have been in education, the sector has touted a commitment to inclusion. Yet despite our incredible efforts, there are certain groups of students not benefiting from school: neurodivergent learners, students with disabilities, and other marginalized groups. Review these alarming statistics (National Center for Learning Disabilities & Understood, 2019) as we begin to unpack this pressing concern.

- Seventy percent of teachers believe they cannot be successful in supporting students with mild to moderate learning disabilities.
- Over 80% of teachers don't feel prepared to teach students with mild to moderate learning disabilities.
- Fifty percent of teachers don't believe students with disabilities can learn grade-level standards.

I firmly believe in our ability to improve these statistics. However, it will require urgent action, a shift in thinking about who's responsible for leading the effort, and a shift in our approach to school design. Six principles can guide leaders in shifting this paradigm (see Table 2.1).

The Status Quo Is Troubling

We'll dive into the six principles momentarily, but before doing so, let's establish the current state, or the status quo. We are all becoming increasingly aware of student and teacher dissatisfaction with school. In recent conversations, I've heard words like "boring," "uninspiring," "irrelevant," "unimaginative," and "isolating." Ask an educator the same question, and you'd likely hear the same thing. Ask a student in special education that same

TABLE 2.1 The Six Principles of a Truly Inclusive School

Principle	Call to Action	Description
Anti-Exclusionary Program Design	Design for marginalized learners.	Academic, behavior, and data policies, practices, and protocols are grounded in inclusive values and purposefully designed to promote growth for students across the spectrum of ability.
Inclusive Professional Learning	Empower all educators to understand learner variability.	Professional learning activities designed to empower all educators to create inclusive learning environments that promote belonging and academic success for all learners.
Person-First Culture	Reframe discipline systems as social-emotional support systems.	An approach to behavior and discipline that promotes a welcoming and affirming environment designed to foster safety, belonging, and well-being.
Student-Centered Instruction	Disrupt general education so all kids can learn.	An academic approach designed to drive growth for all learners by prioritizing and intensely supporting the individual needs, strengths, and differences of each student.
Data Urgency	Collect data frequently and respond immediately.	Emphasizes the immediate and consistent collection of data to allow educators to respond swiftly to student needs.
Collective Responsibility	Commit to being a part of the solution, no matter your role.	Educators must breakdown silos and take joint responsibility for the growth of all learners.

question, and you'd probably hear something even more alarming. A quick scan of social media would reveal countless personal accounts, news stories, and memes evidencing these sentiments.

What Students Are We Talking About?

So, who exactly are we talking about? Let's break down the numbers. U.S. public schools enroll approximately 6.5 million students with disabilities (National Center for Education Statistics, 2023) across 13 disability categories, 5.3 million English learners (National Center for Education Statistics, 2024a), and 1 million students with Section 504 plans (U.S. Department of Education,

TABLE 2.2 Formal Categories for Students Receiving Targeted Supports

Category	Description
Student with a disability (U.S. Department of Education, n.d.)	A student formally evaluated and designated as having 1 of 13 disability classifications that require formal special education services. High-incidence disabilities are those most prevalent disabilities and represent a higher number of students (speech and language impairment, specific learning disability, other health impairment, autism, emotional disturbance). Low incidence disabilities represent a smaller proportion of students with disabilities (blindness, low vision, deafness, hard of hearing, deaf-blindness, multiple disabilities, orthopedic impairment, traumatic brain injury; University of Kansas, 2008).
Student with a 504-plan (U.S. Department of Education, n.d.)	A student with a mental or physical impairment substantially limiting one or more life activities who is provided accommodations or modifications to support their needs.
Multilingual learner (U.S. Department of Education, n.d.)	A student whose home language is not English and requires additional language instruction to promote academic success.
Historically marginalized	Students from all aforementioned groups who are historically marginalized. In addition, this group includes racial/ethnic minorities, students from low socioeconomic backgrounds, and homeless students. This group is defined as students who face compounded challenges that stem from their marginalized identities, impacting their educational opportunities and outcomes. Addressing these disparities requires targeted policies and practices to ensure equity and inclusion in educational settings.

2018). From this point forward, in this book, I will use the term "exceptional learners" to represent the group of students holding these formal labels (see Table 2.2). Use of this phrase is intentional and intended to promote a student-centered view of students who commonly have reduced access to the highest quality supports necessary to support sufficient academic or social-emotional growth.

While these specific identifiers are necessary for the purpose of ensuring that schools are compliant with providing additional support, they are "othering" in day-to-day practice, our goal is to go beyond labels and identify ways to reimagine our systems to meet all of their needs.

One important note: *This book is NOT just about disability. It's about all students who need something better because the design of school is flawed.*

Big Investments, Same Outcomes

The field has invested millions of dollars and developed countless initiatives to support these students, yet outcomes for certain students have not substantively improved over the past 30 years (Keyworth, 2020). While there are pockets of improvement and few bright spots, holistically, students with disabilities, English language learners, and at-risk learners continue to fail to meet expectations (National Center for Education Statistics, n.d.). In fact, the gap between their performance and their general education peers has remained statistically the same, or in some cases worsened, over the past 15 years (see Table 2.3).

Special education and other specialized supports are supposed to promote growth for students, but the data show that isn't happening on a broad scale. Special education has become a place where students go and stay, with no truly meaningful plan that enables them to progress toward their most rigorous postsecondary opportunity. These stagnant outcomes have a detrimental impact on postsecondary success for all students, but especially students with significant disabilities, with many not achieving or maintaining meaningful employment or postsecondary education opportunities (Taylor et al., 2020).

Certain Students Face Extra Hurdles

There are certain students at risk for harsher outcomes, students like my son. I became a teacher because of the harrowing statistics on how exceptional learners were performing in school. These statistics first came to my attention when my son's first-grade

TABLE 2.3 National Assessment of Education Progress. Twenty-Year Performance Analysis of Achievement Gap Between Subgroups and General Education Students (National Center for Education Statistics, 2024b)

Subgroup	Reading Gap						Math Gap					
	2003			2022			2003			2022		
Grade levels	Grade 4	Grade 8	Grade 12	Grade 4	Grade 8	Grade 12	Grade 4	Grade 8	Grade 12	Grade 4	Grade 8	Grade 12
Student with a disability	−35	−41	−45*	−40	−36	−39*	−22	−39	−39*	−28	−36	−35*
English learner	−33	−41	−39*	−31	−38	−52*	−22	−37	−30*	−23	−36	−42*
Eligible for NSLP	−28	−25	*	−28	−23	*	−23	−23	*	−26	−27	*

teacher wanted to refer him to special education because he was "fidgety." As a new law school graduate with no background in education, I did some research, here's what I found:

- Black students, boys, and students with disabilities are disciplined at disproportionately higher rates than their peers (United States Government Accountability Office, 2018a, 2018b).
- Black students are about twice as likely as white students to be suspended (2018).
- Black students with disabilities are more likely than white students with disabilities to be identified as having an emotional disturbance (Bal et al., 2019) or an intellectual disability.
- Academic outcomes for students with disabilities are dismal.

Twenty years later, the statistics remain practically unchanged. Numerous factors, including bias, stereotypes, and other systemic issues, continue to lead to poor outcomes and harsh treatment for certain students. Some researchers note that in urban settings, issues related to leader and teacher bias, segregated programming, the challenge of creating inclusive classrooms, difficulty hiring teachers committed to inclusion, and a lack of cultural competency are also at play (DeMatthews et al., 2021). These issues could serve as fodder for a multipart series, but any further detail is beyond the scope of this book. However, for our purposes, I will highlight two important themes as they recur throughout this book.

- School-wide academic and behavior systems (policies, practices, and protocols) are not designed to support learner variability.
- Educators lack sufficient knowledge, skills, and expertise to support learner variability.

This articulation of the problem really stands out to me:

> Children of color with disabilities do not just experience discrimination as children of color or as children with disabilities, but as both. This type of discrimination is intersectional because it does not simply layer racism on top of ableism. Instead, it is a form of discrimination all its own that deserves specific analysis and tailored remedies.
>
> (2019)

When you combine those characteristics and consider students of color with emotional disabilities, the disparities are compounded. Some researchers espouse that when a student of color also has a disability label, it positions them as inferior to their white peers and their nondisabled peers of color, regardless of whether they have a disability (DeMatthews et al., 2021).

Consider these additional statistics:

- Students with disabilities are suspended at more than double the rate of students without disabilities (Skrtic et al., 2021).
- Triple the number of black students versus white students with disabilities who are removed from class for the same disciplinary offense (U.S. Department of Education, Office of Special Education and Rehabilitative Services, 2021).
- Black male students in special education from low-income families are disproportionately suspended compared to all other subgroups (National Center for Learning Disabilities, 2020).
- Black girls are disproportionately suspended as compared to their representation in the general student population (Wriston & Duchesneau, 2023).

> "Children of color with disabilities do not just experience discrimination as children of color or as children with disabilities, but as both."

To support your journey in cultivating equity in your context, take a moment to reflect on these statistics and the role you can play in disrupting them.

> **MITIGATING DISPROPORTIONALITY**
>
> *Reflect:*
> - *Review the statistics in Table 2.4.*
> - *Brainstorm potential solutions for at least one statistic and outline your role in developing solutions.*

TABLE 2.4 Disproportionality Statistics for Students with Disabilities and Students of Color

Statistic	Potential Barriers to Change	Solution
Students of color with disabilities are disproportionately placed in self-contained classrooms (Hinds et al., 2022) *and* receive insufficient support to promote meaningful academic progress (Bal et al., 2019).	◆ Reduced access to grade-level instruction ◆ Lack of access to content experts ◆ Insufficient behavior goals ◆ General educators lack expertise in effective academic and behavior support for exceptional learners	◆ Integrate effective supports within general education setting ◆ Build educator capacity in supporting learner variability in academics and behavior ◆ Prioritize the development of effective inclusive classrooms
Black children with disabilities are at higher risk for receiving stigmatizing disability labels such as ID, ED, and DD (Hinds et al., 2022).	◆ Negative biases and stereotypes ◆ Lack of culturally responsive systems	◆ Systems for recognizing and mitigating bias ◆ Bias training ◆ Create culturally responsive academic and behavior systems
A diagnosis of emotional disturbance has negative effects on the education and life outcomes for students of color (Bal et al., 2019).	◆ Negative biases and stereotypes ◆ Lack of culturally responsive systems ◆ Behavior systems are punitive and not supportive	◆ Develop proactive and positive approaches to student behavior ◆ Build educator capacity on effective behavior support ◆ Create culturally responsive behavior systems

(Continued)

TABLE 2.4 (CONTINUED) Disproportionality Statistics for Students with Disabilities and Students of Color

Statistic	Potential Barriers to Change	Solution
Many caregivers of color see special education as a tool to segregate their children (Ferri & Connor, 2005).	♦ Negative biases and stereotypes ♦ Lack of culturally responsive systems	♦ Systems for recognizing and mitigating bias ♦ Bias training ♦ Create culturally responsive academic and behavior systems ♦ Prioritize the development of effective inclusive classrooms

The Problems: Knowledge, Ownership, and Design

Now that we've examined the data illustrating the status quo, let's explore potential reasons why outcomes remain stagnant, barriers persist, and solutions remain elusive. My experience, research, and current trends reveal three critical challenges: *knowledge, ownership, and school design*. Examining these areas can lead to potential solutions.

Problem 1: The Knowledge Deficit

Teachers and leaders are not sufficiently prepared to create inclusive schools. They lack sufficient training and have limited experience in supporting students with disabilities (Bettini et al., 2022; Billingsley et al., 2022; National Center for Learning Disabilities and Understood, 2019), multilingual learners, and

TABLE 2.5 Problems Perpetuating the Status Quo for Exceptional Learners

The Knowledge Deficit
Educators lack the necessary knowledge and skills needed to drive strong academic and behavioral outcomes for exceptional learners.

The Ownership Problem
Accountability for outcomes is fragmented, often resting with individuals without the authority to implement system-wide changes necessary to improve outcomes.

The Design Flaw
School learning environments are not structured to promote academic success, a sense of belonging, and social-emotional well-being for exceptional learners.

other exceptional learners. This knowledge deficit contributes to exclusionary practices (DeMatthews et al., 2021) and their corresponding dismal outcomes. If we are to create schools that work for all students, it must become standard practice that every educator has the requisite mindset, knowledge, and skills necessary to create inclusive academic and behavioral systems. Recently, I had a conversation with the founding principal of a nationally recognized inclusive elementary school who said, "When I started this school, I didn't realize it would be *the* school that my own kid needed." My immediate thought was, "Every kid should have access to a school like this, yet this kind of school is reserved for the select few lucky enough to enroll." She was able to create this kind of school because of her inclusive mindset, knowledge, experience, and willingness to learn what she didn't know. This does not represent the average principal's experience. Addressing the knowledge deficit is critical, urgent, and long overdue. In Chapter 6, I outline the essential knowledge and skills needed to build *truly* inclusive schools.

Stop Saying It If You Don't Mean It or Understand It — Equity, Inclusion, and Other Jargon

One way we perpetuate the knowledge deficit is not having a universally accepted usage of terms like *inclusion* and *equity*. Now more than ever, it is critical that we collectively embrace and commit to a shared vision for inclusion and equity. Failure to do so will have far-reaching consequences that will continue to perpetuate the status quo for our most vulnerable students. These concepts have become jargon in practice, and their authenticity in schools varies significantly.

So, what is equity? Equity is *active*. It is an *active process* of seeking justice for all marginalized groups through systemic and transformational change. In schools, equity is commonly thought of in terms of race and ethnicity, but in many cases, those efforts minimize or exclude a focus on achievement for exceptional learners (students with disabilities, students with 504 plans, and multilingual learners). In his latest book, *Fix Injustice, Not Kids*, Paul Gorski, a preeminent voice in the equity conversation, defines equity as the adoption of "specific actions that redistribute access and opportunity" (Gorski & Swalwell, 2023) and is also an "active process for intentionally cultivating justice (including racial justice, disability justice, and economic justice)." Another prominent researcher, David DeMatthews, urges us to extend our description of inclusion, specifically as it relates to inclusive leadership. He suggests that the leadership imperative is not just striving to be *an inclusive leader* but to become an inclusive *and* socially just leader (2021). Being inclusive and socially just requires action by proactively challenging "all forms of exclusion, marginalization, and injustice."

This pursuit of social justice and equity doesn't just sit with school leaders. We cannot significantly shift the status quo for exceptional learners without the partnership of organizations that support schools. These organizations must expand their equity efforts to be intentionally inclusive of exceptional learners across *all* priorities and initiatives. Despite stated commitments to equity, many organizations within the philanthropic community, nonprofit school partners, and other national equity-focused entities lack meaningful and substantive commitments to exceptional learners. Even among organizations with emerging priorities in support of these students, in many cases, they remain as separate initiatives that do not go far enough. These organizations generally lack the necessary priorities, initiatives, and internal expertise to ensure their efforts are having a meaningful impact on the unique needs of exceptional learners.

There is also an opportunity for philanthropy to play a greater role. Many education nonprofits rely on philanthropic support to drive and inform their priorities. Unfortunately, disability justice has not been a top priority in the funding space. In fact, only 2% of the $37 billion in philanthropy supports disability efforts in education (Disability & Philanthropy Forum, 2023).

Disability advocates are calling on philanthropy to

1. be a greater catalyst for disability justice,
2. proactively support the removal of barriers to participation, and
3. work to dismantle systemic ableism.

School support organizations, leadership development programs, and educator preparation must also evolve their equity efforts to become intentionally inclusive of exceptional learners. There are several prominent national leadership fellowship programs delivering content that has significant gaps or wholly excludes any focus on ensuring leaders meaningfully consider exceptional learners. Two commonly known national programs, particularly within the charter school sector, Relay Graduate School of Education's *Inclusive Schools Leadership Institute* and *All Means All*, were founded because of this gap. These programs often attract school leaders who have already participated in prior fellowships or training, which can result in capacity overload and overwhelm for leaders.

Truly living a stated commitment to equity asks these programs to shift to an intentional integration of *effective* inclusive practices in *all* aspects of their content and not operate siloed or add-on programs. Organizations and universities can look to the work of Arizona State University (ASU) and Georgia State University (GSU) as inspiration for how to integrate a focus on exceptional learners in their existing programming. As a part of their participation in the Advancing Inclusive Principal Leadership (AIPL) initiative in partnership with the Council for Chief State School Officers, a statewide team from Georgia, including state-level leaders, committed to meaningful efforts to strengthen principals' ability to lead effective inclusive schools. GSU was a member of the statewide team and focused on strengthening leadership preparation. Their efforts prioritized integrating inclusive practices across all leadership coursework as opposed to a single course, which is common in leadership preparation (CEEDAR Center, 2023). I was one of several statewide coaches supporting the AIPL initiative focused on working with states to develop a vision and strategy for inclusive principal leadership.

At ASU, their education leadership team is currently undergoing a curriculum redesign focusing on the exact same goal. This level of intentionality is the essence of inclusive programming. Such intentional efforts can reduce educator overwhelm and financial strain on systems and schools because they will no longer have to fund add-on training programs and costly secondary supports for students.

The same is true in schools: if you don't have anyone on your leadership team with decision-making authority who has expertise in inclusive education, what do you think will happen? Will you have an inclusive school by osmosis or wishful thinking? No. Without leadership possessing a commitment to and expertise in inclusive education, you will likely never truly meet the call for inclusive schools. Supporting stakeholders (e.g., philanthropy, nonprofits) can start by considering questions such as, "How might the design of our priorities, initiatives, or school-wide systems be unfairly harming or disproportionately benefiting one group, and how can we change this?"

Are You Equity Literate?

In addition to understanding education theory and pedagogy, justice-oriented leaders must also know how to and actively seek to disrupt inequity. To do so, they must be equity literate. Again, considering the broad group of "marginalized learners" is not sufficient, schools and stakeholders must specifically work to consider exceptional learners. The Equity Literacy Framework is useful in helping leaders build this orientation. According to this framework, equity-oriented leaders need *equity desire, equity knowledge, equity skills, and equity will* (Gorski & Swalwell, 2023).

- **Equity desire** represents an individual's aspiration or want to achieve justice for those who have been marginalized.
- **Equity knowledge** is the understanding of injustice, how it operates within systems, and what it looks like within a system (e.g., understanding ableism and how it shows up in schools).
- **Equity skills** reflect a leader's ability to strategically address inequity in a way that is effective and transformative. Being an effective equity leader requires five skills, referred to as the *equity abilities*—the ability to recognize inequity, respond to inequity, redress inequity, cultivate equity, and sustain equity.

- **Equity will** is the *commitment* to actively work for equity and justice (2023).

These four constructs—desire, knowledge, skill, and will—are a useful and concrete way to conceptualize why the status quo persists for students with disabilities. If you surveyed the educators at your school and asked them the following four questions, how do you think they would respond?

- Do you want justice for exceptional learners?
- Do you understand ableism and how it shows up in a school's systems?
- Do you know how to strategically address ableism to transform outcomes for exceptional learners?
- Are you committed to combating ableism and promoting anti-ableism in your context?

I entered the principalship with an orientation toward inclusive education and equity because of my background as a special education teacher and leader. This is not typical for most leaders. If you don't have a natural orientation toward inclusion, meaning you are always thinking through the lens of equity for exceptional learners, you must intentionally work to build that orientation. To support this goal, throughout this book, we will periodically zoom in on the *five equity abilities* in the context of academic, behavioral, and data systems so that you are empowered to create and lead equitable systems for exceptional learners and disrupt inequity when it exists. This process will give you the opportunity to practice that.

Everyone Can't Have Their Own Definition of Inclusion

For our purposes, my definition of *inclusive schools* will be grounded in the goal of belonging and the recent work of prominent researchers on inclusive education (McLeskey et al., 2022a). They define effective inclusive schools as "places where students with disabilities are valued and active participants and where they are provided supports needed to succeed in the academic, social, and extra-curricular activities of the school" (2022a) ***and*** experience success. Schools that have experienced this success focus on the following:

- **Comprehensive Supports.** Includes ongoing and essential services needed to meet the needs of a diverse range of students.
- **Community Investment.** The entirety of the school community supports inclusion and equity for all students.
- **Joint Participation.** Students are educated together during academic and nonacademic activities.
- **Prioritize General Education Placement.** Students are educated in highly effective natural settings that meet their needs resulting in a reduction in placements in separate settings.
- **Collaboration.** Professionals collaborate to provide support and effective instruction.
- **Aligned and Outcomes-Based.** Supports meet individual needs and learner outcomes.

However, inclusion can no longer be the bar. The bar is belonging. Inclusion simply means you are *present* in the community. Belonging exists when students experience meaningful academic and relational experiences as active members of the community; it is a more rigorous bar.

Is your approach aligned with this more rigorous view of inclusion, or are you operating by the status quo definition? Moving beyond the status quo will require leaders to not just build knowledge but also evolve their perspectives. Doing this work through a shared understanding of inclusive schools and practices is an essential first step.

Problem 2: The Ownership Challenge

A wise mentor once told me, "Our world is not binary, and we can't have schools that are binary." We all can agree that there aren't just two kinds of students in our schools. Yet, the existence of the label "student with a disability" assumes two categories of kids, "normal" and "not normal." There are many different identities within a community, and school systems need to be transformed to support those differences. The *ownership challenge* facing schools is that accountability for outcomes is fragmented, often resting with individuals without the authority to implement system-wide changes necessary to improve outcomes. Principals must take the lead in driving change toward inclusive schools by addressing the intersectional forces that are creating oppressive systems (DeMatthews et al., 2021).

The Ownership Challenge: Accountability for academic achievement and social-emotional well-being of exceptional learners is siloed. Improving these outcomes requires the owner and designer of school-wide systems to lead the charge. Principals, superintendents, and other chief-level leaders hold this power and must commit to the responsibility of wielding it to actively promote justice for exceptional learners.

Approximately 70% of students with disabilities spend over 80% of their time in general education classrooms (National Center for Education Statistics, 2024c), yet general education teachers don't hold a corresponding level of responsibility for their academic and social-emotional growth. Many of them also express doubt about their ability to be effective with these learners (National Center for Learning Disabilities & Understood, 2019).

Let's take a moment to think about this more concretely. Consider this classroom:

- 25 students
- 3 students with math learning disabilities
- 2 students with dyslexia
- 1 general education teacher
- 1 special education teacher

Assigning the special educator to the eight students while the general education teacher focuses on everyone else seems fair, right? The problem with this is that there are other factors to consider:

- How does the design of the general educator's lesson cause barriers to engagement or understanding?
- Who has the expertise needed to scaffold and remediate grade-level math standards?

- Does the special educator's full schedule allow them to provide the intensive academic support these students need?
- Is the design of the reading and math block aligned with the needs of these students?

Addressing this challenge requires a shift from siloed supports to a focus on collective responsibility. This shift starts with you. Designing lessons that work for gifted learners and those with learning needs, intentionally designing classroom environments suitable for students from those with autism to those who are gifted and talented, and implementing policies that ensure no group is disproportionately disadvantaged are all examples of a *difference-centered school* AND can only happen when ownership is shared.

Reflect: Consider the *ownership challenge* in your context.

- Who is responsible for academic and behavioral outcomes for exceptional learners?
- Do those individuals hold the requisite knowledge and skills necessary to drive strong outcomes for those learners?
- What do your answers reveal about the ownership challenge in your school, and might that be impacting the performance of your exceptional learners?

Problem 3: The Design Flaw

Many schools are still clinging to traditional classroom design and programmatic structures that are not compatible with the needs of today's students, especially exceptional learners. In my visits to hundreds of classrooms, the most common setup I have observed is students sitting in desks in rows, listening to the teacher standing in the front of the room. The traditional design of school prioritizes efficiency and compliance with norms.

The authors of *Schools for All Kinds of Minds* share this sentiment and note that school environments have remained

> "Our world is not binary. We can't have schools that are binary."

unchanged for over 40 years and that "[t]he future of education calls for entirely new learning environments" (Barringer et al., 2010). One common challenge with the shift to inclusive classrooms is that schools commonly place students in the general education classroom without modifying its design. The pace remains fast, curricular materials are not redesigned, the special educator role isn't strategically redesigned, general educators aren't sufficiently knowledgeable on designing for learner variability, the list goes on. Special educators are tasked with figuring out how to make their students fit in, as opposed to a collaborative team working to figure out how to make the system work for the students.

Design Flaw: You're Doing Too Much, Initiative Overwhelm
Another element of the design problem is the expectation that leaders are doing too much by trying to simultaneously implement multiple equity-focused initiatives—PBIS, SEL, RTI, MTSS, ESS, RTT, and CCSS. What an overwhelming list of acronyms. This list represents commonly used education frameworks and a corresponding set of daunting and unrealistic expectations contributing to the already challenging job of school leadership. This is especially true when frameworks are viewed as disparate programs rather than practices integral to student success. Leaders are left with figuring out which to use, when, and for what purpose, resulting in frustration and/or implementation failure (McIntosh et al., 2016).

In this book, the elements of these frameworks are not addressed in isolation. They are strategically integrated throughout the principles outlined in each chapter, allowing you to develop a nuanced understanding of how their individual practices support inclusive academic and behavioral systems, as opposed to focusing on the title of the framework. This strategic integration is supported by researchers who have proposed a cross-pollination of Universal Design for Learning and Culturally Sustaining Pedagogy because combined, they address and outline critical ways to support "intersecting and compounding forms of exclusion" for students historically marginalized by schools (Podlucká, 2020; Waitoller & Thorius, 2016).

Design Flaw: Designed for the "Average" Learner

Academic settings place numerous cognitive demands on students, posing challenges for the *so-called average learner* and especially for those with intensive needs in the neurodevelopmental domains of attention, memory, higher-order thinking (HOT), language, and social cognition. Table 2.6 outlines five

TABLE 2.6 Neurodevelopmental Domains of Learning (Barringer et al., 2010)

Domain	*Indicators of Strength* (If This System is Strong, Students Can)	*Common Demands of School*
Attention	◆ Maintain and regulate cognitive energy and alertness over a learning period ◆ Process and sort incoming information ◆ Planning, organizing, and producing output at an appropriate pace	◆ Listening to lectures ◆ Completing independent work ◆ Turning in assignments on time
HOT	◆ Make connections across content areas ◆ Interpret and make sense of new ideas ◆ Make inferences ◆ Engage in creative thinking ◆ Engage in systematic problem-solving	◆ Completing projects or experiments ◆ Completing assignments ◆ Analyzing texts and problems
Language	◆ Process and understand oral and written information (receptive language) ◆ Communicate and produce ideas orally and in writing (expressive language)	◆ Following instructions ◆ Completing written assignments
Memory	◆ Store and retrieve information (long-term memory) ◆ Mentally juggle information while using it (working memory)	◆ Remember historical facts ◆ Remember math facts, procedures, and rules
Social Cognition	◆ Navigate interactions with peers ◆ Respond appropriately during social settings ◆ Interpret others' emotions ◆ Collaborate with peers	◆ Working in small groups ◆ Participating in class discussions ◆ Interacting during extracurriculars ◆ Group projects

neurodevelopmental domains that can help educators understand the unique learning profiles of students (Barringer et al., 2010). The reality is that we all vary in each of these domains, and as adults, we develop strategies for self-management and self-regulation, but students who are still growing in these areas need learning environments designed to support that growth.

Consider your own strategies for engaging with this book: coffee, snacks, a quiet space, or listening via audiobook. The use of these strategies aligns with a need in at least one of the neurodevelopmental domains (see Table 2.6). Take a moment to review each domain and circle the indicators that were supported by your chosen strategies.

NEURODEVELOPMENTAL DOMAINS

Reflect:
1. *What does this make you think about the classrooms in your school?*
2. *Is there a mismatch between how your students might vary across these domains and the design of your school's learning environment?*

If there is a mismatch, addressing it is crucial. One way to do this is to shift to a liberatory and student-centered design where schedules, resource allocation, classroom environment, and adult roles and responsibilities mirror student needs, aspirations, and growth goals.

Design Flaw: A Conditions Problem

One element of the design problem is a mismatch between the common structures and policies within schools and the characteristics of inclusive education. Recent research reveals that inclusive practices are not being broadly or consistently implemented in classrooms across the United States (McLeskey et al., 2022b). Leaders I have coached claim a primary barrier to effectively implementing inclusive practices are structures and policies related to scheduling, time usage, hiring practices, usage of staff, and educator capacity.

Supporting students with needs in any of the neurodevelopmental domains requires the strategic design of systems for academics and behavior. Review Table 2.7, an extended version of Table 2.6, "Neurodevelopmental Domains of Learning." This extended version includes an added column outlining conditions necessary for students who may have needs in each area. **Review the last column and answer the following**:

- If a student has a need in this area, these are the conditions necessary for their success. Which conditions are misaligned with the traditional school design?
- Reflect on your own school's structures: How well do they align with these conditions?
- What changes are needed to support the varying needs of your students?

TABLE 2.7 Neurodevelopmental Domains for Learning and Supportive Strategies

Domain	Indicators of Strength (If This System Is Strong, Students Can)	Common Demands of School	Conditions of a Supportive Learning Environment (Scheduling, Usage of Time, Hiring, Staffing)
Attention	◆ Maintain and regulate cognitive energy and alertness over a learning period ◆ Process and sort incoming information ◆ Planning, organizing, and producing output at an appropriate pace	◆ Listening to lectures ◆ Completing independent work ◆ Turning in assignments on time	◆ Academic blocks broken up into bite-sized chunks ◆ Embedded breaks ◆ Flexible academic blocks ◆ Schedule designed around small-group instruction ◆ Schedule that embeds extended time

(Continued)

TABLE 2.7 (CONTINUED) Neurodevelopmental Domains for Learning and Supportive Strategies

Domain	Indicators of Strength (If This System Is Strong, Students Can)	Common Demands of School	Conditions of a Supportive Learning Environment (Scheduling, Usage of Time, Hiring, Staffing)
HOT	◆ Make connections across content areas ◆ Interpret and make sense of new ideas ◆ Make inferences ◆ Engage in creative thinking ◆ Engage in systematic problem-solving	◆ Completing projects or experiments ◆ Completing assignments ◆ Analyzing texts and problems	◆ Flexible scheduling to allow for in-depth exploration of topics ◆ Interdisciplinary teaching teams
Language	◆ Process and understand oral and written information (receptive language) ◆ Communicate and produce ideas orally and in writing (expressive language)	◆ Following instructions ◆ Completing written assignments	◆ Integrate language support into academic blocks ◆ Collaborative planning to integrate language support strategies into lessons
Memory	◆ Store and retrieve information (long-term memory) ◆ Mentally juggle information while using it (working memory)	◆ Remember historical facts ◆ Remember math facts, procedures, and rules	◆ Time in schedule to support review and additional practice ◆ Schedule designed around small-group instruction

(Continued)

TABLE 2.7 (CONTINUED) Neurodevelopmental Domains for Learning and Supportive Strategies

Domain	Indicators of Strength (If This System Is Strong, Students Can)	Common Demands of School	Conditions of a Supportive Learning Environment (Scheduling, Usage of Time, Hiring, Staffing)
Social Cognition	♦ Navigate interactions with peers ♦ Respond appropriately during social settings ♦ Interpret others' emotions ♦ Collaborate with peers	♦ Working in small groups ♦ Participating in class discussions ♦ Interacting during extracurriculars	♦ Allocate time for social skills groups ♦ Implement flexible seating

Design with Students at the Center

Resolving these challenges starts with putting the system user at the center. Our "users" in the school context are not a monolith, so let's stop designing our school-wide systems as if they are. To help strengthen your understanding of learner variability and ability to design systems through an inclusive, we will ground our exploration of the six principles in this book in three sample student profiles (see Figure 2.1) representative of students whose needs fit outside of the "traditional learner." You will revisit these profiles in the remaining chapters and consider how each principle can be applied to support their needs.

THE LEARNER PROFILES

Reflect: Select one student profile from Figure 2.1 and answer both questions.
1. Why might this student struggle in a typical classroom?
2. What will it take to remove barriers to their success?

Learner Profiles

Shawn

- Resilient and motivated learner
- Has dyslexia (struggles with spelling and reading fluency)
- Experiences low mood, anger, and defensiveness
- Thrives in a positive and supportive environment

Isaiah

- Strong long-term memory and motivated to learn
- Requires structure, routines, and positive reinforcement
- Has Autism (uneven cognitive skills, stimming, and repetitive behaviors)
- Lagging skills in emotional regulation (managing frustration)

Darryl

- Highly motivated, independent worker who grasps complex concepts well
- Proficient in reading, math, and science
- Has ADD (fidgets and seeks touch stimulation)
- Resilient and collaborative learner

FIGURE 2.1 Learner Profiles for Tailored Instruction. This figure presents profiles of three diverse learners—Shawn, Isaiah, and Darryl—highlighting their strengths, challenges, and specific needs.

What Caused These Problems, and Why Do They Persist?

We've now taken the time to think about three problems contributing to the status quo, chronically low performance for exceptional learners. Let's start to unpack why they persist. I believe that one reason the status quo remains is because of a focus on school improvement rather than transformation. In a recent meeting led by the Center for Learner Equity, representatives from the Department of Education asked, "What do educators need to improve outcomes for students with disabilities?" My response was, "We keep developing solutions that don't address the root cause of the problem." Outlined in Table 2.8 are potential root causes of each problem and which of this book's six principles offers a solution.

> **THE THREE PROBLEMS**
>
> *Reflect*: *Review Table 2.8 and answer both questions.*
> 1. *Which challenge is most evident in your context?*
> 2. *Which challenge has been most impacted by your leadership? In what ways?*

TABLE 2.8 Root Causes of the Knowledge, Ownership, and Design Problems

Problem	Potential Root Causes	Impact	Solution
The Knowledge Deficit	◆ Educator prep and professional learning lacking integration of inclusive practices across all programs	◆ General education teachers and leaders lack understanding of learner variability and how to design supportive academic and behavioral systems ◆ Teacher coaching and support systems are siloed	Inclusive Professional Learning (Principle 4) Collective Responsibility (Principle 6)
	◆ Expertise around social cognition and effective behavior support primarily held by specialists	◆ Discipline systems and policies are punitive and reactive	Person-First Culture (Principle 2)
	◆ Special education teacher preparation lacks adequate focus on academic content knowledge	◆ Students with disabilities lack sufficient access to high-quality grade-level and specialized instruction	Inclusive Professional Learning (Principle 4)
	◆ Special educator roles, responsibilities, and schedules are not optimized for effectiveness or student growth	◆ Teacher burnout ◆ Teachers focus on compliance versus academic outcomes	Anti-Exclusionary Program Design (Principle 1)

(Continued)

TABLE 2.8 (CONTINUED) Root Causes of the Knowledge, Ownership, and Design Problems

Problem	Potential Root Causes	Impact	Solution
The Ownership Challenge	♦ General educators lack expertise in designing for learner variability	♦ Instruction is not designed to support learner difference ♦ Academic blocks are not designed to support learner difference	Inclusive Professional Learning (Principle 4) Student-Centered Instruction (Principle 3)
	♦ Hiring and scheduling prioritizes efficiency	♦ Students with disabilities are excluded from general education	Anti-Exclusionary Program Design (Principle 1)
The Design Flaw	♦ Accountability systems exclude rigorous growth and proficiency expectations for exceptional learners ♦ Knowledge of inclusive school design is siloed	♦ Supports for exceptional learners are provided in segregated settings ♦ Educators maintain low expectations for students with disabilities ♦ Exceptional learners receive insufficient academic supports	Data Urgency (Principle 5) Inclusive Professional Learning (Principle 4) Collective Responsibility (Principle 6)

Review Table 2.8 to further examine the three problems related to knowledge, ownership, and school design. Your reflection will guide you in navigating the principles in this book and developing a plan for systemic change in your school.

In the face of persistent challenges and systemic failures within the educational landscape, exacerbated by the disruptive impact of the COVID-19 pandemic, there is an urgent need to empower educators with the necessary tools and resources to create inclusive schools and classrooms. These challenges include the following:

- Increased academic setbacks, with more students falling behind grade level.
- Greater variation in academic performance within classrooms makes it challenging for teachers to address all students' needs.
- Rising behavioral and mental health challenges among students.

We can mitigate these challenges by focusing on inclusive systems, changing perspectives on responsibility, and committing to an evolved vision of equity. Redesigning classrooms with inclusive education at the foundation can be a solution for all students.

Now that we've unpacked three potential problems perpetuating the status quo for exceptional learners, let's dive into *Principle 1: Anti-Exclusionary Program Design* and examine the foundational elements of building an inclusive school.

Bibliography

Bal, A., Betters-Bubon, J., & Fish, R. E. (2019). A multilevel analysis of statewide disproportionality in exclusionary discipline and the identification of emotional disturbance. *Education and Urban Society*, 51(2), 247–268.

Barringer, M.D., Pohlman, C., & Robinson, M. (2010). *Schools for all kinds of minds: Boosting student success by embracing learning variation.* Jossey-Bass.

Bettini, E., Mathews, H.M., Lillis, J., Meyer, K.M., Shaheen, T., Kaler, L., & Brunsting, N.C. (2022). The role of teachers in effective inclusive elementary schools. In J. McLeskey, N. L. Waldron, F. Spooner, & B. Algozzine (Eds.), *Handbook of effective inclusive elementary schools* (2nd ed., pp. 43–76). Routledge.

Billingsley, B., DeMatthews, D., Raab, R.R., & James, L. (2022). Principal actions in effective inclusive schools: a review of elementary case studies. In J. McLeskey, N. L. Waldron, F. Spooner, & B. Algozzine

(Eds.), *Handbook of effective inclusive elementary schools* (2nd ed., pp. 16–42). Routledge.

Campbell, J. (1999). *Student Discipline and Classroom Management*. Charles C Thomas Publisher, Ltd.

CEEDAR Center. (2023). Advancing Inclusive Principal Leadership: State Policy and Practice. University of Florida. Retrieved from https://ceedar.education.ufl.edu/wp-content/uploads/2023/08/final-2-1-21-.pdf

Copeland, S. R., & Cosbey, J. (2009). Effective instructional practices to support the inclusion of students with extensive support needs in general education classrooms. *Research and Practice for Persons with Severe Disabilities*, 33(4), 214–227.

Courtade, G., Jimenez, B., Root, J., & Pennington, R. (2022). Planning for effective inclusive instruction in core content. In J. McLeskey, N. L. Waldron, F. Spooner, & B. Algozzine (Eds.), *Handbook of effective inclusive elementary schools* (2nd ed., pp. 286–301). Routledge.

DeMatthews, D. E., Serafini, A., & Watson, T. N. (2021). Leading inclusive schools: Principal perceptions, practices, and challenges to meaningful change. *Educational Administration Quarterly*, 57(1), 3–48.

Disability & Philanthropy Forum. (2023). Foundation Giving for Disability: Priorities and Trends. Source: https://disabilityphilanthropy.org/wp-content/uploads/2023/02/FoundationGivingForDisability_FullReport.pdf

DuFour, R., DuFour, R., Eaker, R., Many, T., & Mattos, M. (2016). *Learning by doing: A handbook for professional learning communities at work* (3rd ed.). Solution Tree Press.

Endrew, F. ex rel. Joseph F. v. Douglas Cty. Sch. Dist. RE-1, 137 S. Ct. 988 (2017).

Ferri, B. A., & Connor, D. J. (2005). "Tools of exclusion: Race, disability, and (re) segregated education." *Teachers College Record* 453–474. https://www.researchgate.net/publication/249400367_Tools_of_Exclusion_Race_Disability_and_Resegregated_Education

Fleming, J. I., Grasley-Boy, N. M., Gage, N. A., Lombardo, M., & Anderson, L. (2024). Effects of Tiered SWPBIS Fidelity on Exclusionary Discipline Outcomes for Students With Disabilities: A Conceptual Replication. *Journal of Positive Behavior Interventions*, 26(1), 3–13. https://doi.org.ezproxy4.library.arizona.edu/10.1177/10983007231193173

Fritz, R., & Harn, B. (2022). Effective literacy instruction in inclusive schools. In J. McLeskey, N. L. Waldron, F. Spooner, & B. Algozzine (Eds.), *Handbook of effective inclusive elementary schools* (2nd ed., pp. 199–220). Routledge.

Fullan, M. (2016). *Coherence: The right drivers in action for schools, districts, and systems*. Corwin Press.

Gorski, P., & Swalwell, K. (2023). *Fix injustice, not kids and other principles for transformative equity leadership*. ASCD.

Grant, A. (2023). *Hidden potential: The science of achieving greater things*. Viking.

Griffin, C., Kwon, J.B., Apraiz, K., & Wong, L.N. (2022). Creating opportunities for struggling mathematics learners in inclusive schools. In J. McLeskey, N. L. Waldron, F. Spooner, & B. Algozzine (Eds.), *Handbook of effective inclusive elementary schools* (2nd ed., pp. 221–244). Routledge.

Hammond, Z. (2015). *Culturally Responsive Teaching and The Brain: Promoting Authentic Engagement and Rigor Among Culturally and Linguistically Diverse Students*. Corwin.

Heath, C., & Heath, D. (2010). *Switch: How to change things when change is hard*. Crown Business.

Hinds, H., Newby, L. D. T., & Korman, H. T. N. (2022). Ignored, punished, and underserved: Understanding and addressing disparities in education experiences and outcomes for Black children with disabilities. Bellwether Education Partners & Easterseals. https://www.bellwether.org

Implicit bias and teacher diversity: when will schools push for change? (2020). In University Wire. Uloop, Inc.

Individuals with Disabilities Education Act (IDEA), 20 U.S.C. § 1400 (2004).

Kelly, J., & Pohl, B. (2018). Using Structured Positive and Negative Reinforcement to Change Student Behavior in Educational Settings in order to Achieve Student Academic Success. *Multidisciplinary Journal for Education, Social and Technological Sciences*, 5(1), 17–29. https://doi.org/10.4995/muse.2018.6370

Keyworth, R. (2020). Overview of national achievement tests. The Wing Institute. https://www.winginstitute.org/student-national-standardized-tests

Kurth, J. A., Miller, A. L., & Toews, S. G. (2020). Preparing for and Implementing Effective Inclusive Education with Participation Plans. *Teaching Exceptional Children*, 53(2), 140–149. https://doi.org/10.1177/0040059920927433

Lewis, C. W., & Toldson, I. (Eds.). (2013). *Black male teachers: Diversifying the united states' teacher workforce*. Emerald Publishing Limited.

Lin, L., Parker, K., & Horowitz, J. M. (2024). Problems students are facing at public K-12 schools. Pew Research Center. https://www.pewresearch.org/social-trends/2024/04/04/problems-students-are-facing-at-public-k-12-schools/

McIntosh, K., Kelm, J. L., & Canizal Delabra, A. (2016). In search of how principals change: A qualitative study of events that help and hinder administrator support for school-wide PBIS. *Journal of Positive Behavior Interventions*, 18(2), 100–110. https://doi.org/10.1177/1098300715599960

McLeskey, J., Maheady, L., Billingsley, B., Brownell, M. T., & Lewis, T. J. (2022a). *High leverage practices for inclusive classrooms* (2nd ed.). Routledge.

McLeskey, J., Waldron, N. L., Spooner, F., & Algozzine, B. (2022b). Time to support inclusion and inclusive schools. In J. McLeskey, N. L. Waldron, F. Spooner, & B. Algozzine (Eds.), *Handbook of effective inclusive elementary schools* (2nd ed., pp. 3–13). Routledge.

Minahan, J., & Rappaport, N. (2012). *The behavior code: A practical guide to understanding and teaching the most challenging students*. Harvard Education Press.

National Center for Education Statistics. (2023, TBA). Table 311.10. Number and percentage distribution of students enrolled in postsecondary institutions, by level, disability status, and selected student characteristics: Academic year 2019–20 [Data table]. In Digest of education statistics. U.S. Department of Education, Institute of Education Sciences. https://nces.ed.gov/programs/digest/d22/tables/dt22_311.10.asp

National Center for Education Statistics. (2024a). English Learners in Public Schools. Condition of Education. U.S. Department of Education, Institute of Education Sciences. https://nces.ed.gov/programs/coe/indicator/cgf

National Center for Education Statistics. (2024b). NAEP assessments. U.S. Department of Education, Institute of Education Sciences. https://nces.ed.gov/nationsreportcard/assessments/

National Center for Education Statistics. (2024c). Students with Disabilities. Condition of Education. U.S. Department of Education, Institute of Education Sciences. Retrieved May 30, 2024, from https://nces.ed.gov/programs/coe/indicator/cgg

National Center for Education Statistics. (n.d.). NAEP assessments. U.S. Department of Education, Institute of Education Sciences. https://nces.ed.gov/nationsreportcard/assessments/

National Center for Learning Disabilities. (2020). Significant disproportionality in special education: Current trends and actions for impact. https://www.ncld.org/sigdispro

National Center for Learning Disabilities & Understood. (2019). Forward together: Helping educators unlock the power of students who learn differently. National Center for Learning Disabilities. https://www.ncld.org

National Council on Teacher Quality. (2020). Content Knowledge National Results. State Teacher Policy Database. [Data set]. https://www.nctq.org/yearbook/national/Content-Knowledge-92

Patti, A.L., Rafferty, L.A., Budin, S., & Maheady, L. (2022). The role of high leverage practices in effective elementary inclusive schools. In J. McLeskey, N. L. Waldron, F. Spooner, & B. Algozzine (Eds.), *Handbook of effective inclusive elementary schools* (2nd ed., pp. 181–198). Routledge.

Podlucká, D. (2020). Transformative Anti-Ableist Pedagogy for Social Justice: Charting a Critical Agenda for Inclusive Education. Outlines. *Critical Practice Studies*, 21(1), 69–97. https://doi.org/10.7146/ocps.v21i1.118234

Rojewski, J. W., Lee, I. H., & Gregg, N. (2013). Causal effects of inclusion on postsecondary education outcomes of individuals with high-incidence disabilities. *Journal of Disability Policy Studies*, 25(4), 210–219. https://doi.org/10.1177/1044207313505648

Simonsen, B. & George, H.P. (2022). Supporting inclusive practices with positive behavioral interventions and supports. In J. McLeskey, N. L. Waldron, F. Spooner, & B. Algozzine (Eds.), *Handbook of effective inclusive elementary schools* (2nd ed., pp. 139–163). Routledge.

Skrtic, T. M., Saatcioglu, A., & Nichols, A. (2021). Disability as status competition: The role of race in classifying children. *Socius*, 7, Article 23780231211024398. https://doi.org/10.1177/23780231211024398

Taylor, J. L., & Sailor, W. (2023). A case for systems change in special education. *Remedial and Special Education*, 45(2), 125–135. https://doi.org/07419325231181385

Taylor, J. P., Rooney-Kron, M., Whittenburg, H. N., Thoma, C. A., Avellone, L., & Seward, H. (2020). Inclusion of students with intellectual and developmental disabilities and postsecondary outcomes: A systematic literature review. *Inclusion*, 8(4), 303–319. https://doi.org/10.1352/2326-6988-8.4.303

Tyack, D., & Cuban, L. (1995). *Tinkering toward utopia: A century of public school reform*. Harvard University Press.

U.S. Department of Education. (n.d.-a). English learner (EL) characteristics. https://www2.ed.gov/datastory/el-characteristics/index.html

U.S. Department of Education. (n.d.-b). Statute: Chapter 33, Subchapter I, Section 1401. https://sites.ed.gov/idea/statute-chapter-33/subchapter-i/1401

U.S. Department of Education, Office for Civil Rights. (2018). Estimations from the Civil Rights Data Collection, 2017–2018. https://civilrightsdata.ed.gov/estimations/2017-2018

U.S. Department of Education, Office for Civil Rights. (n.d.). Frequently asked questions about Section 504 and the education of children with disabilities. https://www2.ed.gov/about/offices/list/ocr/504faq.html

U.S. Department of Education, Office of Special Education and Rehabilitative Services. (2015, November 16). Dear Colleague Letter on Free Appropriate Public Education (FAPE).

U.S. Department of Education, Office of Special Education and Rehabilitative Services. (2021, August). OSEP fast facts: Race and ethnicity of children with disabilities served under IDEA Part B. https://sites.ed.gov/idea/osep-fast-facts-race-and-ethnicity-of-children-with-disabilities-served-under-idea-part-b/

United States Government Accountability Office. (2018a). K-12 education: Discipline disparities for Black students, boys, and students with disabilities (GAO-18-258). https://www.gao.gov/products/gao-18-258

United States Government Accountability Office. (2018b). K-12 education: Discipline disparities for Black students, boys, and students with disabilities (GAO-18-258). https://www.gao.gov/products/gao-18-258

University of Kansas. (2008). Low-incidence versus high-incidence disabilities. https://educationonline.ku.edu/community/low-incidence-versus-high-incidence-dis-abilities

Waitoller, F. R., & Thorius, K. A. K. (2016). Cross-pollinating culturally sustaining pedagogy and universal design for learning: Toward an inclusive pedagogy that accounts for dis/ability. *Harvard Educational Review*, 86(3), 366–389. https://doi.org.hoover2.mcdaniel.edu:2443/10.17763/1943-5045-86.3.366

Whole Child Model. (n.d.). Homepage. https://www.wholechildmodel.org

Williams, Ereka R. Unnecessary and Unjustified: African-American Parental Perceptions of Special Education. *The Educational Forum* (Spring 2007): 250–261.

Wriston, B., & Duchesneau, N. (2023). How school discipline impacts students' social, emotional, and academic development (SEAD).

3

Principle 1

Anti-Exclusionary Program Design

The call to action for leaders is to:
Design for marginalized learners

Old Thinking: *We fit exceptional learners into existing systems and create add-on programs if the system doesn't meet their needs.*
New Thinking: *We actively dismantle barriers and transform systems to promote belonging and academic growth for exceptional learners.*

In This Section

Transforming outcomes for exceptional learners will require leaders to reimagine their overall approach to program development and systems design. Systems design must actively respond to the needs of exceptional learners, remove barriers to their success, and actively promote their academic and social-emotional growth—systems must be *anti-exclusionary*. This chapter outlines the five core practices of anti-exclusionary program design: public commitment, systems transformation, collaborative design, human-centered resource allocation, and needs-based innovation (DeMatthews et al., 2023; Holmes, 2018). These are the foundational beliefs and decision-making guidelines that should inform policies, practices, and protocols. Let's dive in.

CHAPTER CONTENTS

♦ Defining Anti-Exclusionary
♦ Core Practices: Anti-Exclusionary Program Design
♦ From Knowing to Doing: Driving Change for Anti-Exclusionary Program Design
♦ Anti-Exclusionary Habits
♦ Tips for Parents
♦ Your Role
♦ Action Planning

Defining Anti-Exclusionary

In our schools, we are comfortable failing certain groups of students. In the last chapter, I shared data that illustrates the inability of schools to systemically promote positive academic or behavioral outcomes for students who are neurodivergent, students with disabilities, and other exceptional learners. The call to action is to redesign programs with the needs of these students at the forefront. In other words:

Design for marginalized learners.

It is likely that everyone reading this book believes in equity for all learners. But are your systems designed to promote equity for *all* learners, not just "most" or "some?" Promoting equity for all learners will require schools to center marginalized students in the design of school-wide systems, which will likely require a shift in your approach to policy development, the design of your protocols, the selection of instructional practices, who you hire, and how you leverage human capital.

Building inclusive anti-exclusionary schools requires leaders to understand and actively work to combat attitudes, policies, and practices that disregard or marginalize individuals with disabilities and other exceptional learners—such policies and practices are defined as ableist. Leaders can work toward the creation of anti-ableist or anti-exclusionary environments by centering marginalized students in systems design.

Despite our long-standing efforts toward inclusive schools, meaningful and transformative changes for the broader disability population remain elusive. Adopting a more substantive perspective of anti-ableism, as activist Talila Lewis proposes, is a crucial next step. To help us envision a new perspective, Lewis offers the following expanded definition of ableism:

> A system that places value on people's bodies and minds based on societally constructed ideas of normality, intelligence, excellence, desirability, and productivity. These constructed ideas are deeply rooted in anti-Blackness, eugenics, misogyny, colonialism, imperialism, and capitalism.
>
> This form of systemic oppression leads to people and society determining who is valuable and worthy based on a person's language, appearance, religion and/or their ability to satisfactorily [re]produce, excel and "behave."
>
> You do not have to be disabled to experience ableism.
> (Lewis, 2021)

Lewis emphasizes that anti-ableist efforts must extend beyond achieving justice for individuals with disabilities (2021). Inclusion advocates can leverage this definition as a tool to better engage leaders and other key decision-makers who have historically de-prioritized efforts for students with disabilities. With that in mind, I offer this definition of anti-ableism as inspiration for the six principles laid out in this book:

> *Anti-ableism is an active effort to dismantle systems and beliefs that unfairly value people based on socially constructed ideas of normality, intelligence, and productivity. An anti-ableist approach to systems design embraces policies, practices, or*

procedures that actively promote inclusivity for everyone regardless of appearance, ability, language, or other subgroup classification.

So, why isn't this chapter titled "Anti-Ableist Program Design?" In my work with leaders, I have found that when leaders can see a practice is beneficial to a broader group of students, they are more likely to buy into the practice or idea. So, I offer "anti-exclusionary" as the principle to provide a broader application of the term. Here's the idea: if leaders are intentional about creating systems that work for students who are historically *excluded*, chronically underperforming, overlooked, or segregated because of an identity marker (e.g., gifted and talented, disability, race)—by designing at the margins—they create more robust systems that meet the needs of a wider range of students. This act of designing at the margins includes five key elements: public commitment, systems transformation, collaborative design, human-centered resource allocation, and needs-based innovation (DeMatthews et al., 2023; Holmes, 2018). The next section describes those five elements (Table 3.1).

TABLE 3.1 Core Practices of Anti-Exclusionary Program Design

Core Practice	*Description*
Commit and Catalyze an Inclusive Vision	Establish shared inclusive values and commit to actively fostering an inclusive environment that proactively promotes belonging and strong academic outcomes for exceptional learners.
Transform the "Big 3" Systems	Restructure and align all school-wide systems, policies, and practices to reflect and uphold the values of inclusivity.
Collaborative Design	Actively involve diverse stakeholders in the design and decision-making processes to ensure systems are inclusive.
Human-Centered Resource Allocation	Allocate resources to prioritize the unique needs of each student, ensuring that funding, materials, and support services are distributed to align with the vision for inclusivity.
Needs-Based Innovation	See student challenges as an opportunity for creating innovative solutions that transform educational systems to better meet their needs.

Anti-Exclusionary Program Design: Core Practices

Core Practice 1: Commit and Catalyze an Inclusive Vision

Description: *Establish shared inclusive values and commit to actively fostering an inclusive environment that proactively promotes belonging and strong academic outcomes for exceptional learners.*

Most schools operate from a set of values that can be found in their public-facing collateral. Yet, in many cases, those values are not reflected in the day-to-day actions of educators nor in how exceptional learners are supported in schools. Making the shift toward being "actively committed," or anti-exclusionary, requires leaders to ensure their stated values *actively* guide adult and student expectations, systems design, and student supports. There is a common thread among schools actively working toward or effectively supporting exceptional learners. They operate by shared values underpinning their success—collective accountability, productive rigor, acceptance, inclusive professional learning, and inclusion-first instruction.

Collective Accountability: "Every Kid Is My Kid"

This value represents the belief that exceptional learners are the collective responsibility of all educators. In inclusive schools, the academic and behavioral success of exceptional learners is the responsibility of all educators, not just specialists. Accountability starts with ensuring educators have the knowledge and expertise needed to effectively support exceptional learners. All adults must also be accountable for understanding how to support the diverse student types in a classroom. To make this a reality, leaders must proactively create opportunities to build their own and others' specialized knowledge about how to effectively support learner variability. This includes providing the necessary support (e.g., time, training, and resources) reflective of a commitment to inclusive practices.

Many schools believe they are inclusive, yet their systems for accountability and expectations are not reflective of that belief. Existing teacher evaluation and recognition systems allow teachers and schools to achieve the highest reward rating even if none

TABLE 3.2 Snapshot of Urban District's Proficiency Guidelines for Students with Disabilities

Grade-level	Reading (average percentage of students with disabilities expected to achieve proficiency)	Math (average percentage of students with disabilities expected to achieve proficiency)
Elementary	8	10
Middle	9	5
High School	7	1

of their students with disabilities meet proficiency standards. Table 3.2 provides a snapshot of one state's accountability framework outlining the proficiency standards for students with disabilities. This is an example of a lack of accountability, given the low threshold for the number of students expected to achieve proficiency.

There is no disagreement that the goal of proficiency for students with disabilities is complex and remains elusive. Leading researchers warn, "The average achievement gap we identified should alarm parents, educators, policymakers, and others with interest in the academic outcomes of SWDs" (Gilmour et al., 2019). Providing the intensive support needed to meet the academic needs of exceptional learners is challenging, but maintaining low expectations provides no impetus or incentive for meeting this challenge. However, until we have an alternative measure, their results must be considered. Accountability for their outcomes results in increased access and participation (McLaughlin & Rhim, 2007).

As a counterexample, one recognition system that does require accountability for students with disabilities is the U.S. Department of Education's National *Blue Ribbon Award*. To receive this award, schools must be ranked as high-performing overall *and* meet the corresponding standard of excellence for the academic achievement of all subgroups, including students with disabilities (U.S. Department of Education, n.d.). The Rhode Island Educator Evaluation system (Holdheide, 2013) is another example of progress, as the new system was intentionally designed with students with disabilities in mind. Specifically, teachers are required to set targeted goals for subgroups and must ensure no subgroup is disproportionately excluded. Additionally, general educators are accountable for ensuring students with disabilities achieve mastery and make appropriate progress (2013).

Schools striving to become inclusive schools can increase *collective accountability* by creating systems for accountability that extend the responsibility of planning for and the performance of exceptional learners across role types. Here are some examples:

- All teachers and leaders are accountable for the academic growth of exceptional learners in the classrooms they support.
- Evaluation and reward systems hold teachers accountable for the academic growth of exceptional learners they support.
- Collaborative team meetings include intentional planning for exceptional learners, with the next steps assigned to both special and general education teachers and leaders.
- In co-taught classrooms, both teachers support exceptional learners and general education students.
- All general educators participate in professional learning activities that build their expertise in supporting the needs of exceptional learners.
- Educators receive coaching, feedback, reflection, and action planning focused on their ability to effectively support exceptional learners.

Acceptance: "I Understand You, And You Matter"

This value represents the belief that student differences should be respected and valued by all. As U.S. schools become increasingly diverse, including in terms of disability, it's crucial to view each difference as a unique learning pathway rather than reasons to separate or marginalize students. Vygotsky taught us to view a student's disability not as a deficiency but as an alternative development route (Gindis, 1999). Educators should actively consider ability, culture, ethnicity, and other identity markers in the development of systems, policies, and practices.

Here are some examples of what it looks like when a school exemplifies this value:

- Exceptional learners and their parents articulate a sense of belonging across all aspects of the school setting.
- Student cultural backgrounds and identities are viewed as assets.
- Texts, materials, and instructional practices reflect the diversity of all students.
- Educators receive professional learning opportunities to build their cultural competence and understanding of learner variability.
- Students with disabilities are meaningfully included in extracurricular activities with their nondisabled peers.
- Student decision-making discussions include student success or strengths.
- Students are not excluded in any way that makes them feel dejected or singled out.
- Students with behavioral challenges are not ostracized, but their challenges are viewed as social-emotional needs, and educators work to proactively support their needs.

(Fritzgerald, 2020; Gay, 2010; Hammond, 2015; Ladson-Billings, 1995; Leverson et al., 2021)

Inclusion-First Instruction: "Every Student Deserves to Be In"

This value focuses on the belief that exceptional learners are entitled to meaningful opportunities to receive their primary instruction in an inclusive setting. Students with disabilities are legally entitled to instruction in the least restrictive environment, and the general education classroom should be the default placement for the student (Billingsley et al., 2022). However, there is a misconception that students with disabilities are better served when they receive their primary instruction in an alternative setting such as a resource classroom, self-contained classroom, or specialized school. Research does not support this notion.

Research shows that students, even those with extensive support needs, perform better in highly effective inclusive general education settings (2022). Designing inclusive instructional systems is addressed in greater detail later in this book.

Here are indicators of inclusion-first instruction.

- ◆ The general education teacher incorporates strategies to mitigate potential barriers to engagement, understanding, or expression in lesson plans.
- ◆ The instructional model supports meaningful instruction for exceptional learners (e.g., co-teaching, small-group instruction, peer-assisted instruction, use of assistive technology, adapted curricular resources, flexible grouping).
- ◆ General education teachers are implementing accommodations and modifications as required by individualized education plans.
- ◆ Exceptional learners maximally participate in activities with their general education peers.

Rigor for All: "Every Student Deserves and Needs a Challenge"

Receiving instruction within the general education is just a first step. The content students engage in also matters greatly. Rigorous academic opportunities are often neglected in the design of academic experiences for exceptional learners. While they are entitled to meaningful access to rigorous grade-level content, lack of access and low expectations for this group of students continue to persist and prevent exceptional learners from reaching their highest potential (Griffin et al., 2022). Exceptional learners can meet grade-level expectations when given appropriate services and supports, meaning reasonably designed to provide access to grade-level standards (Endrew, 2017).

Teachers can increase access by designing lessons that promote learner interest and motivation, support understanding by using multiple modalities, and provide students with multiple options to demonstrate understanding (i.e., universally designed instruction). This should *then be* combined with appropriate accommodations and modifications aligned to each student's individual learner profile and research-based intervention in areas of concern by content experts (Fritz & Harn, 2022). This combination of instructional supports is what defines "meaningful access to rigorous grade-level content."

Indicators of this value include the following:

- Students with the highest level of need receive instruction from highly effective teachers with content expertise in their area(s) of need.
- Remedial instruction does not replace standards-based, grade-level instruction.
- Exceptional learners have rigorous academic goals that are aligned with individual student needs and designed to fill instructional gaps as quickly as possible.
- The general education teacher incorporates strategies in lesson plans to mitigate potential barriers to engagement, understanding, or expression.
- The instructional model supports meaningful instruction for exceptional learners (i.e., co-teaching, small-group instruction, peer-assisted instruction, use of assistive technology, adapted curricular resources, and flexible grouping).
- Exceptional learners maximally participate in activities with their general education peers.

Each of the aforementioned values is fundamental in supporting the success of exceptional learners. Let's begin our journey toward catalyzing inclusivity by reflecting on our individual values and identifying ways in which we can work to better embody them in our own roles and contexts. Reflect by reading the following student story and answering one of the questions that follow.

Student Story—Thasya

PROVOKING QUESTION: What would be the impact if we measured our schools by their ability to effectively include and promote belonging for students like Thasya?

Imagine a third-grade classroom where a nonverbal student with autism is thriving; she has friends, plays with her nondisabled peers at recess, and is an inspiration to other classrooms. I'd like to introduce you to that third-grade student, Thasya. I first learned about Thasya when I was designing the inclusive leadership program I founded in 2017 after watching the short film *Thasya*, produced by Dan Habib. When Thasya first started attending Maplewood Elementary, the school highlighted in the film, she was nonverbal and exhibited challenging behaviors. Some of those behaviors included frequent meltdowns when there were unexpected changes or schedule adjustments. Thasya's journey toward success began by identifying her interests as a tool to foster engagement within the classroom.

Recognizing a need to increase and build her communication skills, her team introduced a communication device that proved to be a game-changer. As the entire team became proficient in its use, Thasya's progress was remarkable. She not only demonstrated increased verbal communication but also experienced a reduction in negative behaviors and improved collaboration with her peers. Thasya's inclusion not only positively impacted her own growth but also impacted her classmates and peers throughout the school, who, over time, eagerly sought her out for play during recess. Serving as her primary advocate, Thasya's classroom teacher possessed a deep understanding of her unique needs and played an instrumental role in her success. Although working with a student like Thasya presented new challenges, the school team embraced the mindset of "we will find a way" and committed to the journey together.

EXAMINE YOUR BELIEFS

Reflect: Choose <u>one</u> question to answer.
1. Which value is most evident in Thasya's story? What does this make you think about your own context?
2. Does your leadership align with the five inclusive values? How is this impacting the experience of your exceptional learners?

Core Practice 2: Transform the "Big 3" Systems
Description: Restructure and align all school-wide systems, policies, and practices to reflect and uphold the values of inclusivity.

What Is a System? The "Big 3"

Creating inclusive schools requires leaders to employ the five inclusive values to shape expectations, policies, practices, and protocols across all systems. Let's start our examination of systems transformation by defining the term "systems" and exploring their significance in creating an inclusive environment. Within a school, there are three major systems that drive the student experience. I categorize them as the "Big 3": data, culture, and instruction. While a school's overall operations are necessary to bring these systems to life, this book primarily focuses on the "Big 3" because they are key drivers that shape students' experiences, foster growth, and cultivate a strong sense of belonging.

In her book *Punished for Dreaming*, Bettina Love urges us to recognize how traditional school reform efforts have particularly harmed students of color and those from other marginalized communities (Love, 2023). Love calls for a responsive effort that includes accountability, truth-telling, cessation, healing, *and* transformation. Similarly, Gorski and Swalwell, in *Fix Injustice, Not Kids*, and the authors of *Schools for All Kinds of Minds*, urge us to engage in active efforts that transform existing systems to both improve outcomes and eliminate their harmful impacts. This starts with aligning academic, behavioral, and data systems to a shared commitment to inclusivity. Each "system" is comprised of policies, processes, and structures that drive the day-to-day student experience (see Table 3.3).

The Instructional System. The system at the core of the day-to-day routines within a school is the instructional system. This includes the elements of a school's program that facilitate student learning—pedagogical approaches, teaching strategies, curriculum design, and planning. Traditional characteristics of an instructional system may include classroom layouts with desks in rows facing the front of the classroom, lecture-based instructional methods emphasizing direct instruction, uniform

TABLE 3.3 The "Big 3" Systems and System Elements

	System Elements	
System	Policies and Protocols	Collaboration Structures
Culture	♦ Discipline policy ♦ School-wide behavior management system ♦ Classroom rules and routines ♦ Progress monitoring ♦ Social-emotional learning	♦ Behavior team meetings ♦ Student support team meetings ♦ Data step-back meetings
Instruction	♦ Curriculum ♦ Planning tools and protocols ♦ Teaching methods (e.g., lectures, group discussions, project-based learning) ♦ Coaching ♦ Academic block (schedule and routines, e.g., intervention, small-group instruction)	♦ Grade-level team meetings ♦ Intellectual preparation ♦ Lesson planning
Data	♦ Data collection and analysis protocols ♦ Assessment administration protocol ♦ Progress monitoring systems	♦ Weekly data meetings ♦ Interim assessment data meetings ♦ Data step-back meetings

curriculum delivery, standardized assignments for all students, or rigid instructional blocks where students are expected to do the same thing at the same time. My work with leaders across the United States has shown that many of these elements are extremely common in schools and are not supportive of the diversity of our classrooms. *Principle 4* of this book outlines the specific practices within an inclusive instructional system: *Tiered Instruction, Universally Designed Grade-Level Instruction, Personalized Learning Structures, Targeted Interventions, and High-Quality Specialized Instruction.*

The Culture System. The components within a school that drive the relational, behavioral, and emotional experience for students and staff encompass the culture system. A school's culture is driven by the day-to-day rituals, routines, and rules that guide student and adult behavior. These systems are critical because they impact and influence student character, well-being, and safety. Traditional culture systems are characterized as behavior or discipline systems, but in this book, they will be classified as *social-emotional support systems* (see Principle 3). This is intentional, as their purpose should be to promote student well-being and safety instead of being punitive. Reframing systems for discipline and behavior as social-emotional support systems is a more student-centered approach and can foster a more inclusive culture.

The Data System. All components within a school that include the collection, analysis, and utilization of student performance data to improve instructional practices make up its data system. A robust data system involves tracking and analyzing formal and informal assessment results, attendance records, discipline data, and other relevant metrics to gain insights into student progress and make informed adjustments. Many educators express overwhelm and frustration with the amount of data they are expected to collect and articulate concerns about whether certain data types (standardized assessments) provide accurate useful information about student proficiency, especially for exceptional learners. Notwithstanding those criticisms, when it comes to students who have been historically marginalized by schools, the use of meaningful data is essential to inform necessary interventions and determine whether interventions are driving toward improvement.

How to Design Your Systems

Before you continue, let me give a caveat. This is not a long diatribe about MTSS or RTI. MTSS (*Multi-Tiered Systems of Support*) has become one of those jargony "terms" and frameworks that have caused a lot of frustration and debate over the past ten or so years. The simple reality is every principal must understand MTSS because it provides a strategic approach to systems design. **MTSS is not a special education initiative**; it is simply a system for leveraging data to organize student supports; **all schools should be designed around MTSS**.

MTSS is a data-driven, three-tiered approach to service delivery for academics and behavioral supports. At Tier 1, schools provide a universal evidence-based academic program and behavioral supports to *all* students and incorporate additional supports as needed. Educators collect data to determine how students are progressing and use that data to determine who needs additional support and moves into the next tier: Tier 2. Tier 2 describes the intensity of those additional supports. Student response to targeted supports is monitored through strategic data collection, and those who are not responsive receive more intensive support and move to Tier 3 (see Table 3.4).

Typically, 80%–90% of students need Tier 1 support, 10%–15% need Tier 2 support, and 1%–5% need Tier 3. You may have greater numbers of students needing Tier 2 and Tier 3 support, especially if you serve a high-need population, are dealing with the lasting impacts of the COVID-19 pandemic, or are facing increasing concerns around student engagement. Living the

TABLE 3.4 MTSS Overview

Level of Intervention	Academics	Behavior
Tier 1	♦ Evidence-based instruction in content areas ♦ High-quality standards-aligned curriculum ♦ Universal design for learning (design instruction to attend to learner variability in the classroom)	♦ School-wide preventative and positive behavior policy ♦ Clearly defined and taught behavior expectations ♦ Frequent and positive reinforcement of desired behavior
Tier 2	♦ Supplemental academic supports (e.g., small-group interventions, additional practice opportunities, tutoring)	♦ Targeted behavior interventions (e.g., small-group interventions aligned to challenging behavior, check-in/check-out system, behavior contracts in conjunction with skills instruction and support)
Tier 3	♦ More frequent interventions, personalized interventions (1:1) ♦ Referral for additional services	♦ Individualized behavior plans, functional behavior assessment (formal assessment); Targeted behavior interventions are more individualized and intensive (e.g., 1:1 counseling, crisis plans, wraparound services)

promise of MTSS requires an intentional design of schedules, systems, and the use of adults aligned to its structure.

Schools must stop viewing MTSS as "just another initiative" and recognize it as the essential approach for ensuring strategic systems design to effectively respond to all student's unique academic and behavioral needs. Decisions such as integrating social-emotional supports into the design of academic systems or scheduling extended academic blocks to account for students in need of intensive support are the cornerstone of a strategic approach to systems design. This level of intentionality requires the principal to have deep expertise in MTSS and to guide these efforts. While I will not go into extensive detail about MTSS in this book, Chapter 7, "Data Urgency," will help leaders strengthen their understanding of using data in alignment with that framework. Again, the goal is to concentrate on the core practices of data, academic, and behavioral systems — *not* the name of a framework.

Core Practice 3: Collaborative Design

Description: Actively involve diverse perspectives in the design and decision-making processes to ensure systems are inclusive.

Those responsible for policy development, scheduling, and other elements of system design typically are not the same individuals with expertise in inclusive practices. So, by design, these systems are often not inherently inclusive. To be inclusive, individuals with expertise in inclusive education and the needs of exceptional learners should be engaged to cocreate academic, behavioral, and data systems. Meaningfully including these individuals may include engaging them as full members of the leadership team with a shared voice in final decision-making, creating schedules that prioritize their participation in collaborative meetings (e.g., Individualized Education Program (IEP) meetings that they facilitate are not scheduled during leadership team meetings), or developing feedback loops that allow them to provide input on systems design. The Liberatory Design Framework (Anaissie et al., 2021) serves as a useful guide for engaging community members. This framework pushes practitioners to ensure diverse individuals and perspectives are included in design processes and considers this essential to removing barriers and eliminating the existing status quo.

Core Practice 4: Human-Centered Resource Allocation

Description: Allocate resources to prioritize each student's unique needs, ensuring that funding, materials, and support services are distributed in accordance with a vision for inclusivity.

Every school has a vision outlining its hopes and promises for student success, often using inclusive language such as "all students" and "every learner." However, these visions for inclusion are frequently misaligned with how resources are allocated, resulting in unfulfilled promises for many learners, particularly exceptional learners. Allocating resources for efficiency is easier, but it perpetuates long-standing inequities. Schools allocate three primary resources to support their overall program: people, time, and money. Strategic and student-focused allocation of these resources is crucial to meeting the promises of inclusive education (Barakat, 2019; Goldan, 2019). What if we humanized our thinking about resources and reframed their utilization as "human-centered resource allocation?" How might that shift the way we approach hiring, staff assignments, professional learning, scheduling, and budgeting?

Hiring and Staffing

"I hire for will over skill" is the sentiment shared by many inclusive leaders I have collaborated with over the years. These leaders prioritize hiring staff who believe equity is paramount over expertise and experience. Inclusive schools need educators who uphold high expectations for every learner, regardless of identity marker; believe it is their responsibility to support every student; and are willing to be flexible and problem-solve when it comes to figuring out how to meet student needs. Most educators would likely say, "I have high expectations for my students," however, the key is not in what they say but in what they *do*.

Holding high expectations alone will not address this challenge. Leaders must align resources in a way that will meet that challenge. Strategic hiring can be a solution. For example, instead of hiring generalist special educators, leaders should consider hiring and incentivizing reading and math specialists for special education roles and work to build their capacity to understand learner variability.

After hiring, leaders must make decisions about how they utilize staff. A human-centered staff allocation model promotes teacher efficacy and well-being *and* is designed to drive the highest possible student outcomes. This approach means leaders must consider the needs of marginalized and high-need student groups in staffing assignments. I love asking the question, "If a student has a learning disability in math, what expertise does that student's teacher need to help support that student access grade-level standards and remediate skill gaps?" What do you think? Jot down some ideas in the space below.

- _____
- _____
- _____

Here's what I have heard:

- *"They need teachers who understand math content."*
- *"They need teachers who understand learning disabilities in math."*
- *"They need teachers with expertise in math intervention."*

Now look at your list and my list and ask yourself, is this reflective of who we typically hire and assign to support students with learning disabilities in our schools? Here are some alarming facts about staffing:

- Most states don't expect special educators to have content expertise in the subjects they support (National Council on Teacher Quality, 2020).
- Most general education teachers who teach students with math learning disabilities don't think they have the skills needed to support these students (National Center for Learning Disabilities & Understood, 2019).

- Only two states require high-incidence special education teachers to demonstrate sufficient knowledge of the subject matter they are licensed to teach (National Council on Teacher Quality, 2020).
- Only ten states require a sufficient test on whether special education teachers understand the science of reading (2020).

Unless we change our current approach to hiring and staffing, we will maintain the status quo for exceptional learners. Here are some indicators of a human-centered approach to hiring and staffing:

- Students with extensive reading and math challenges receive their primary instruction from teachers with expertise in those areas.
- Staff expertise is aligned with student needs.
- Teacher responsibilities prioritize accountability for student learning (e.g., assign compliance duties to an operational role).
- Staff who lack sufficient expertise to support student needs have targeted professional learning plans (e.g., special educators are assigned to one content area and receive professional development to build content expertise).
- General educators receive professional learning opportunities focused on inclusive practices and understanding learner variability.
- Leadership roles and responsibilities are equitable and promote efficacy for leaders of exceptional learners (e.g., a special education leader is not responsible for coaching all grade levels on effective behavior support and coaching all special education teachers in all content areas).

Use of Time

The school schedule is one of the most important resources a leader controls. It reflects a school's values and priorities because it dictates who gets access to resources and opportunities and who does not. Traditional schedules often fail to ensure students are supported by teachers with the skills best aligned to their needs. I often hear special educators express that their roles are fragmented, with much of their time consumed by tasks that do not directly drive student learning.

An inclusive schedule is the goal and should be designed in collaboration with leaders and teachers of exceptional learners. Exceptional learners need the most out of the school day, and without attending to their needs first, their needs will likely remain unmet. In *The Way to Inclusion*, the authors outline the *Inclusive System Scheduling Process* that provides concrete steps to build an inclusive schedule (Causton et al., 2023).

Here are some key considerations for creating an inclusive schedule:

- Create a schedule that promotes efficacy for special educators (e.g., they aren't responsible for multiple grade levels and content areas in a way that reduces their instructional efficacy or personal well-being).
- Integrate breaks and downtime for staff and students to support their well-being.
- Create a schedule ensuring exceptional learners receive accessible grade-level instruction *and* intervention.
- Extend academic blocks to allow flexibility in pacing, modality of instruction, and sufficient time for small-group instruction.
- Provide opportunities for all students to meaningfully participate in non-academic programming, such as extra-curriculars and field trips.

It's simply not enough to say you have an inclusive vision; you must allocate time, assign and hire people, and spend money in alignment with that vision; failure to do so will lead to minimal impact. Table 3.5 outlines how traditional resource allocation compares to human-centered resource allocation. Review the table and answer the questions that follow.

TABLE 3.5 Resource Allocation Comparison: Traditional vs. Human-Centered

Resource Type	Category	Traditional Approach	Human-Centered Resource Allocation
Human Capital	Hiring	Focus on expertise and experience	Hire for inclusive mindsets and/or expertise in inclusive education
	Staff Roles	Fixed roles; traditional staffing structures	Flexible roles aligning teacher expertise to student needs; shared responsibility
	Professional Development	Infrequent and siloed content	All staff engage in learning about inclusive practices
Scheduling	Academic Blocks	Fixed periods with little flexibility	Flexible pacing and varied instructional modalities
	Special Education Services	Services provided in separate settings	Inclusive instructional model; supports integrated into general education
	Planning	Incompatible schedules; No allocated time for collaborative planning	Consistent and frequent planning time focused on inclusive practices
Usage of Time	Interventions	Scheduled during academic blocks, lunch, or after school	Integrated within regular school day; targeted intervention blocks; receive intervention and grade-level instruction
	Instruction	Focus on lecture and whole-group instruction	Schedule prioritizes small-group instruction, focus on active learning and engagement
	Support Services	Isolated from regular classroom activities	Specialists push into general education classroom; specialists coach teachers
Budgeting	Resource Allocation	Focus on efficiency	Secures and aligns resources to student needs
	Professional Learning	Limited investment in opportunities to learn about inclusive practices for all staff	Ongoing and consistent professional learning and coaching focused on inclusive practices

> **RESOURCE ALLOCATION**
>
> *Reflect:* Choose <u>one</u> question to answer.
> 1. How does your school's current resource allocation reflect a vision for inclusivity? Ground your response in the values listed earlier.
> 2. When should efficiency take precedence? If a leader has to prioritize efficiency, what can be done to ensure marginalized students are not harmed as a result?

Core Practice 5: Needs-Based Innovation

Description: See student challenges as an opportunity for creating innovative solutions that transform educational systems to better meet their needs.

What is your typical response when a student is doing something that conflicts with expectations or differs from what other students are doing? Do you evaluate the system to see if it can be improved, or do you focus on removing the student? Let's consider Thasya, the student highlighted in the "Student Story." Thasya's behaviors and expressive language challenges conflicted with existing classroom expectations. Students like Thasya are typically placed in self-contained classrooms or specialized schools. However, her teacher was committed to including her in the regular lessons with her other students. So, instead of requesting placement into a special classroom, program, or school, Thasya's teacher collaborated with the district team to integrate assistive technology supports into the classroom and incorporate the content of the lesson into Thasya's communication device so that she could participate in the lesson. They also leveraged *Positive Behavior Interventions and Supports* to meet her behavioral needs. They considered Thasya's challenges as an opportunity to innovate their systems. Not only did this benefit her, but it also positively impacted how her students interacted with other students with disabilities in a more welcoming and empathetic way than students in other classrooms.

Often, when students encounter challenges, it stems from a mismatch between the student and their environment or expectations; for example, if a person is in a wheelchair but there is no ramp to enter the building, there is a mismatch between their needs and the design of the building. Similarly, a student with a diagnosed emotional disability might struggle to maintain positive peer relationships, yet teachers design lessons requiring small groups or partners without intentional consideration of this need. When students fail to meet expectations, a typical response is to initiate a consequence, contact a caregiver for additional support, or request a change in the educational placement. An inclusive and equity-centered approach results in educators having a default reaction of, "Is there a mismatch between the student's needs and the environment, *and how might we adjust the environment to increase student success?"*

Imagine a world where instead of assuming that something was wrong with the student, educators defaulted to questioning whether the system design was the problem. In such a world, reimagining the system might not just transform the learning experience for an individual student but can also positively impact others.

Inclusive Systems Checklist

To support educators with envisioning and fostering inclusivity within school-wide systems, I have developed a checklist (Table 3.6) outlining the five core practices of anti-exclusionary program design. This checklist can help leaders envision their systems through a more inclusive lens. Use this checklist to inform the design of policies, processes, and structures within each system or to support a continuous improvement process where educators reflect on how existing systems are meeting your vision for inclusivity.

ANTI-EXCLUSIONARY PROGRAM DESIGN

Reflect: Choose <u>one</u> question to answer.
1. Which core practice seems most transformative?
2. How might you leverage the Inclusive Systems Checklist?

TABLE 3.6 Inclusive Systems Checklist

Element	Look-Fors
Values-Driven	◆ System is rooted in a set of clearly defined inclusive values. ◆ Each participant in the system models and is unapologetic about aligning the system to a shared set of inclusive values. ◆ Student strengths are leveraged to support decision-making. ◆ Leaders celebrate and reinforce those who embody inclusive values. ◆ There is no student group who is disadvantaged because of the system. The needs of exceptional learners are proactively addressed in the system.
Transform the "Big 3" Systems	◆ Leaders demonstrate a commitment to redesigning school systems for inclusion. ◆ The systems are proactively designed to promote academic and social-emotional progress for historically marginalized students. ◆ Systems are realigned to reflect inclusive values. ◆ Policies, processes, and structures within each system are aligned with inclusive values.
Collaboratively Designed	◆ The system design is rooted in collaborative relationships and shared responsibility between general and specialist educators. ◆ All members of the system take collective responsibility for supporting all learners. ◆ Leaders and/or teachers of exceptional learners are not excluded from systems/teams in a way that negatively impacts exceptional learners. ◆ Meetings that target the needs of exceptional learners include general educators and nonsped leaders.
Human-Centered Resource Allocation	◆ Resource allocation prioritizes student needs and goal attainment over efficiency. (Hiring practices, classroom resources, staffing decisions/assignment). ◆ Resources are allocated to ensure that students with the most significant needs receive high-quality resources aligned with their needs (e.g., goal-aligned scheduling, instruction from content experts, physical resources, environment). ◆ Exceptional learners receive supports/practices selected and proven to effectively support exceptional learners. ◆ Decisions are based on the perspective of an inclusive set of stakeholders. ◆ Consider how traditionally marginalized learners will be harmed if you don't make necessary trade-offs.

From Knowing to Doing: Driving Change for Anti-Exclusionary Program Design

As you uncovered in this chapter, creating truly inclusive schools will require leaders to reimagine the overall design of schools. You must have a dual focus—creating schools that work for students AND creating schools that work for educators. Throughout this chapter, you were asked to reflect on your current state and existing barriers and to consider your next steps. Moving forward will require significant change—change in philosophy, expectations, policies, and systems design.

Considerations for change management and improvement science are critical to implementing the core practices throughout this book. This section is arguably the most important part of every chapter. Without considering the principles of change and the enabling conditions necessary to create an anti-exclusionary program, your efforts will likely fall flat. Leaders must avoid the "seductive shortcut" (Dufour et al., 2016), which warns against quick fixes without addressing underlying issues. For example, relying solely on a checklist without applying the skills of an equity-literate leader—recognizing inequity, responding to inequity, redressing inequity, cultivating equity, and sustaining equity (Gorski & Swalwell, 2023)—will perpetuate the existing inequities that caused the undesirable outcome. Applying these five skills is essential for identifying and addressing conditions that cause inequity.

Change toward inclusive education requires technical work and social transformation. For schools, change is even harder due to the busy and urgent nature of day-to-day operations and the challenges faced by educators. Because of this, when trying to bring about significant change, systems frequently revert to stasis or the old way of doing things. To achieve lasting transformation, it is crucial to understand and address the underlying structures and system dynamics necessary to prevent systems from reverting to their previous state (Taylor & Sailor, 2023).

Use Table 3.7 as a guide in your planning as you seek to transform toward an anti-exclusionary program. Every step listed is

TABLE 3.7 Change Management Checklist

Key Steps	Understand and Consider Your Context	Leader Actions
Lay the Foundation	*Identify Your Current State*	♦ Identify factors relevant to your local context (e.g., regulatory limitations, resource availability) that impact your ability to create an inclusive programmatic approach. Δ ♦ Don't allow these factors to be barriers to transforming your systems, but consider them so that your plan is responsive and relevant. ♦ Identify ways to proactively address each factor and develop solutions that support an inclusive vision. ♦ Evaluate how your current approach to program design is reflective of an inclusive and anti-exclusionary approach. ♦ Where there are gaps, evaluate the root causes for each gap. Δ ♦ Identify potential barriers to implementation for each core practice.
	Build Relationships and Trust	♦ Evaluate whether you have the necessary relationships to engage and empower members of your team, staff, and community to drive change in this area. ♦ Identify the next steps for building key relationships and gaining results for your community. Δ
	Engage Your Community	♦ Identify key collaborators from each stakeholder group (teachers, caregivers, students, community members) to be meaningfully involved in the planning and implementation process. Δ ♦ Identify strategies for gathering community input and perspectives to support a sense of ownership and commitment.

(Continued)

TABLE 3.7 (CONTINUED) Change Management Checklist

Key Steps	Understand and Consider Your Context	Leader Actions
Empower Key Stakeholders	Build Capacity	◆ Ensure the entire community knows and understands the criteria for success and their role. ◆ Create a systematic approach to ensuring all educators have the skills needed to implement and sustain the core practices aligned to the focus area.
	Create a Compelling Vision	◆ Develop and communicate a compelling vision that resonates with the values and aspirations of your stakeholders. ∆
	Create Systems of Support	◆ Address the emotional aspects of change. ◆ Be willing to make courageous decisions when there is misalignment.
	Be Driven by Action	◆ Be empathetic and intentional about addressing the concerns of those affected by the change. ◆ Provide necessary resources to support their ability to navigate the change.
Focus on Outcomes	Use Data to Drive Decision-Making	◆ Set clear goals and create an action plan for each of the core practices aligned to your target area. ∆ ◆ The framework in the appendix can be used as a self-reflection tool to guide goal setting.
	Align Policies and Practices	◆ Develop leading and lagging indicators to help monitor success and inform needed adjustments. ∆
Transform Systems	Ongoing Inquiry	◆ Align policies and practices to your vision and your commitment to equity. Relevant policies and practices may include hiring, staffing, scheduling, usage of resources, and design of the school environment. ∆ ◆ Identify how existing policies and practices in this area may be perpetuating inequity. ◆ Eliminate policies and practices that are perpetuating inequity. ◆ Transform systems and resist temporary or band-aid solutions. ∆

(Continued)

TABLE 3.7 (CONTINUED) Change Management Checklist

Key Steps	Understand and Consider Your Context	Leader Actions
Continuous Improvement	Celebrate Success	♦ Create a system for ongoing inquiry to improve practices. Δ ♦ Elicit feedback from impacted stakeholders. ♦ Evaluate whether redesign or new policies and practices are creating or perpetuating inequity for historically marginalized groups. ♦ Be flexible and responsive to feedback. Δ
	Understand and Consider Your Context	♦ Share progress and successes with all stakeholders. ♦ Celebrate wins, milestones, and achievements to motivate staff and build momentum. Δ

(Tyack & Cuban, 1995; Heath & Heath, 2010; DuFour et al., 2016; Fullan, 2016).

crucial and cannot be omitted. To further support your planning process, I encourage you to utilize the *Inclusive Schools Design Journey Tool* linked in the appendix. This online tool helps leaders track progress and integrates the considerations outlined in the table.

Pay special attention to the steps labeled as "critical," as indicated by the symbol "Δ." These steps are integral to systems transformation and will significantly determine your overall success.

This list broadly represents key enabling structures that need to be in place to support inclusive school-wide systems. However, specific structures exist relative to the specific systems of behavior and instruction. The following chapters will outline those specific conditions.

Tips For Parents

Here are some tips for parents who want to strengthen their ability to advocate for their own or other students. Each chapter will include tips that correspond to its principle.

- **Request learning opportunities.** Ask the school to provide learning opportunities for caregivers focused on inclusive practices, learner variability, and co-teaching models.
- **Examine your own beliefs.** Reflect on your own beliefs and practices. Consider how you can support inclusive values at home and advocate for them at school.
- **Learn about anti-ableism.** Understand what anti-ableism means and how it impacts your child's education. Advocate for an anti-ableist approach in your child's school.

Your Role

The call to action for leaders is to:
Design for marginalized learners

Each stakeholder has a crucial role to play in actively creating an anti-exclusionary and inclusive environment where every student can thrive. From principals who set the vision and hold stakeholders accountable to teachers who implement inclusive practices and parents advocating for their child's needs, every individual can play a meaningful part in this effort. Use Table 3.8 to identify actions you can take in answering the call for anti-exclusionary program design.

Action Planning

As we conclude this chapter, we are reminded that creating a *truly* inclusive school requires a shared vision and a collective effort. It is not enough to simply say or integrate the words "equity" and "inclusion" into a vision statement; leaders must authentically embody their meanings and actively work toward their realization. Thasya's story is a powerful reminder of the transformative impact inclusive practices can have on exceptional learners and the entire school community.

TABLE 3.8 Stakeholder Roles

Key Steps	Design for Marginalized Learners
School Leader (Principal, Executive Director, Assistant Principal, etc.)	Ground academic, behavioral, and discipline policies, procedures, and protocols in inclusive values and setting expectations aligned to those values.
Principal Managers and District Leaders	Set a vision for inclusivity, aligning district-wide expectations to an inclusive vision, and allocate resources to support that vision.
Funders	Ensure funding priorities intentionally include exceptional learners by requiring grantee initiatives to intentionally mitigate or remove barriers to promote success for exceptional learners.
School Support Organizations	Ensure all programming and initiatives support schools with improving outcomes for exceptional learners.
Policymakers	Mandate practices that improve outcomes for exceptional learners and create policies or incentives that require schools to intentionally mitigate or remove barriers to promote success for exceptional learners.
Families and Caregivers	Educate yourself about learner variability and model and encourage inclusive attitudes and behaviors.

Complete the prompts in the space below or use the action planning template to outline your next steps for answering this chapter's call to action.

Planning Template

Planning Task	Notes
Final Reflection How has this chapter expanded your view on equity? Revisit your answer to the first reflection question about the three sample learner profiles and respond with those profiles in mind. Which stakeholder role do you hold, and what will you do to commit to the call to action?	
Goal Craft one goal aligned with the content of this chapter.	
Resources What resources are needed to meet this goal? Consider human capital, scheduling, and finances.	

Bibliography

Anaissie, T., Cary, V., Clifford, D., Malarkey, T. & Wise, S. (2021). Liberatory Design. http://www.liberatorydesign.com

Barakat, B. (2019). *Resource allocation for inclusive education: A GEM Report analysis*. UNESCO.

Billingsley, B., DeMatthews, D., Raab, R., & James, L. (2022). Principal actions in effective inclusive schools: A review of elementary case studies. In J. McLeskey, L. Maheady, B. Billingsley, M. T. Brownell, & T. J. Lewis (Eds.), *Handbook of effective inclusive elementary schools* (pp. 16–42). Routledge.

Causton, J., MacLeod, K., & Pretti-Frontczak, K. (2023). *The way to inclusion: How leaders create schools where every student belongs*. ASCD.

DeMatthews, D., Billingsley, B., McLeskey, J., & Cowart Moss, S. (2023). Inclusive principal leadership: Moving toward inclusive and high-achieving schools for students with disabilities (Document No. IC-8b). University of Florida, Collaboration for Effective Educator Development, Accountability, and Reform Center.

DuFour, R., DuFour, R., Eaker, R., Many, T., & Mattos, M. (2016). *Learning by doing: A handbook for professional learning communities at work* (3rd ed.). Solution Tree Press.

Endrew, F. ex rel. Joseph F. v. Douglas Cty. Sch. Dist. RE-1, 137 S. Ct. 988 (2017).

Fritz, R., & Harn, B. (2022). Effective literacy instruction in inclusive schools. In J. McLeskey, N. L. Waldron, F. Spooner, & B. Algozzine (Eds.), *Handbook of effective inclusive elementary schools* (2nd ed., pp. 199–220). Routledge.

Fritzgerald, A. (2020). *Antiracism and Universal Design for Learning: Building Expressways to Success*. CAST Professional Publishing.

Fullan, M. (2016). *Coherence: The right drivers in action for schools, districts, and systems*. Corwin Press.

Gay, G. (2010). *Culturally Responsive Teaching: Theory, Research, and Practice*. Teachers College Press.

Gilmour, A. F., Fuchs, D., & Wehby, J. H. (2019). Are Students with Disabilities Accessing the Curriculum? A Meta-Analysis of the Reading Achievement Gap between Students with and without

Disabilities. *Exceptional Children*, 85(3), 329–346. https://doi.org/10.1177/0014402918795830

Gindis, B. (1999). Vygotsky's Vision: Reshaping the Practice of Special Education for the 21st Century. *Remedial and Special Education*, 20(6), 333–340. https://doi.org/10.1177/074193259902000606

Goldan, J. (2019). Demand-oriented and fair allocation of special needs teacher resources for inclusive education – Assessment of a newly implemented funding model in North Rhine-Westphalia, Germany. *International Journal of Inclusive Education*. https://doi.org/10.1080/13603116.2019.1568598

Gorski, P., & Swalwell, K. (2023). *Fix injustice, not kids and other principles for transformative equity leadership*. ASCD.

Griffin, C., Kwon, J.B., Apraiz, K., & Wong, L.N. (2022). Creating opportunities for struggling mathematics learners in inclusive schools. In J. McLeskey, N. L. Waldron, F. Spooner, & B. Algozzine (Eds.), *Handbook of effective inclusive elementary schools* (2nd ed., pp. 221–244). Routledge.

Hammond, Z. (2015). *Culturally Responsive Teaching and The Brain: Promoting Authentic Engagement and Rigor Among Culturally and Linguistically Diverse Students*. Corwin.

Heath, C., & Heath, D. (2010). *Switch: How to change things when change is hard*. Crown Business.

Holdheide, L. (2013). *Inclusive design: Building educator capacity to support all students*. American Institutes for Research, GTL Center. https://gtlcenter.org/sites/default/files/GTL_Inclusive_Design.pdf

Holmes, K. (2018). Mismatch: How inclusion shapes design. MIT Press; Causton, J., MacLeod, K., Pretti-Frontczak, K., Mancini Rufo, J., & Gordon, P. (2023). *The way to inclusion: How leaders create schools where every student belongs*. ASCD.

Ladson-Billings, G. (1995). Toward a Theory of Culturally Relevant Pedagogy. *American Educational Research Journal*, 32(3), 465–491.

Leverson, M., Smith, K., McIntosh, K., Rose, J., & Pinkelman, S. (2021). 1 PBIS Cultural Responsiveness Field Guide: Resources for Trainers and Coaches. Center on PBIS, University of Oregon. www.pbis.org. March 2021.

Lewis, T. (2021, January). Working definition of ableism. Talila A. Lewis. https://www.talilalewis.com/blog/january-2021-working-definition-of-ableism

Love, B. L. (2023). *Punished for dreaming: How school reform harms Black children and how we heal*. St. Martin's Press.

McLaughlin, M. J., & Rhim, L. M. (2007). Accountability Frameworks and Children with Disabilities: A Test of Assumptions about Improving Public Education for All Students. In *International Journal of Disability, Development and Education* (Vol. 54, Issue 1, pp. 25–49). https://doi.org/10.1080/10349120601149698

National Center for Learning Disabilities & Understood. (2019). Forward together: Helping educators unlock the power of students who learn differently. National Center for Learning Disabilities. https://www.ncld.org

National Council on Teacher Quality. (2020). Content Knowledge National Results. State Teacher Policy Database. [Data set]. https://www.nctq.org/yearbook/national/Content-Knowledge-92

Snyder, R. A., & Pufpaff, L. A. (2021). Current State of High Stakes Teacher Evaluation for Special Education Teachers. *Journal of Special Education Apprenticeship*, 10(1).

Taylor, J. L., & Sailor, W. (2023). A case for systems change in special education. *Remedial and Special Education*, 45(2), 125–135. https://doi.org/07419325231181385

Tyack, D., & Cuban, L. (1995). *Tinkering toward utopia: A century of public school reform*. Harvard University Press.

U.S. Department of Education. (n.d.). Eligibility for the No Child Left Behind Blue Ribbon Schools Program. https://www2.ed.gov/programs/nclbbrs/eligibility.html

4

Principle 2

Inclusive Professional Learning

The call to action for leaders is to:
Empower all educators to understand learner variability.

Old Thinking: *General education teachers and leaders are not responsible for having expertise in supporting exceptional learners.*
New Thinking: *Every classroom includes diverse learners, and understanding learner variability is everyone's responsibility.*

In This Section

As the leader, you are the chief designer of your school. One of your key responsibilities is designing learning environments that meet the needs of students across the spectrum of difference. Do you and the educators in your school understand the neurodevelopmental constructs of memory, language, attention, higher-order cognition, and social cognition, how they affect learning, and what strategies should be used when their functions are not operating as they should? If not, who is your learning environment designed to support?

Inclusive education is fundamentally a social justice issue. Social justice advocates emphasize that disability should be seen as an integral aspect of diversity, challenging traditional notions of "normal." They push for proactive pedagogy, which requires educators to deeply understand and teach disability and differences as essential components of human diversity (Connor, 2014). This understanding is crucial for designing inclusive learning environments that disrupt ableism and address the needs of all students.

Despite the wealth of inclusive education literature, when it comes to effectively supporting exceptional learners, educators often say, "I don't know how." As an inclusive leader, it is your responsibility to ensure that all teachers have the skills needed to support the diverse learners in their classrooms, including students with disabilities (Billingsley et al., 2022; DeMatthews et al., 2023). Chapter 3 introduced the essential dispositions of an inclusive leader, and this chapter outlines the most essential knowledge and skills of an inclusive *learning* leader. Bridging this knowledge gap is critical. This chapter outlines what educators and other stakeholders need to know about learner variability and how to support that variability in schools.

CHAPTER CONTENTS

- Student Story
- People Can't Do What They Don't Know
- What ALL Educators Need to Know About Learner Variability
- Knowledge and Skills to Support Inclusive Classrooms
- Coaches Toolkit

Student Story

PROVOKING QUESTION: *Why do current educator preparation and professional learning efforts fail to empower teachers to succeed with students like Thasya?*

For this student story, let's return to Thasya, whom I introduced in Chapter 1. Thasya was a third-grade student at Maplewood

Elementary School with autism who was nonverbal and exhibited behaviors such as yelling, crying, and throwing. If you watch the SWIFT Center film about Thasya's school experience, one of the most impactful things you'll notice is that the person whose voice you hear most is the general education teacher. She deeply understood Thasya's strengths and needs and how to support her effectively. She understood how to use an augmentative communication device to communicate with Thasya and integrated grade-level curriculum content into the device so that she could engage with her classmates. Maplewood's principal saw the general education teacher as the most pivotal part of Thasya's team and committed to fostering effective collaboration between her and the special education team with the goal of aligning the support she received with what was expected in the regular classroom. In addition to focusing on curriculum access, Thasya's success was contingent upon the team knowing and understanding how to implement positive behavior supports. The impact of including Thasya not only positively impacted her growth but also impacted the other students as they gained a greater ability to empathize with and interact with her and other students with disabilities.

EDUCATOR EXPERTISE

Reflect: What do educators need to know and be able to do to support a student like Thasya? Do the educators in your school possess this knowledge and these skills? What are the implications if they do not?

What *ALL* Educators Should Know About Learner Variability

People Can't Do What They Don't Know

Many advocates for inclusive education expend extensive amounts of energy trying to change hearts and minds; in my experience, most educators are open to the idea of inclusion but don't have the skills needed to make it happen. Equipping educators with the knowledge necessary to create inclusive classrooms can catalyze a change in mindsets (Billingsley et al., 2022). Schools have committed to inclusivity by increasing the number of students with disabilities and other diverse learners within the general education classroom but have remained stagnant in preparing educators to support them (Billingsley et al., 2022; DeMatthews et al., 2023). Thasya's teacher was able to help her because she learned how and had the support needed to do so.

While leaders don't enter the role with expertise in math, reading, gifted education, disability, and every single topic that impacts effective teaching and learning, they are still responsible for ensuring students receive an effective education. Accordingly, leaders must have a strategy for building their own and others' expertise in their areas of need.

Foundational Learning: What Is Learner Variability?

Since learning is a school's core business, it seems logical that educators should understand how students learn. Because learners are not monoliths, educators should also understand how learners vary. This is the concept of learner variability. In *All Kinds of Minds*, the authors introduce a neurodevelopmental framework useful for understanding this variability and creating supportive learning environments.

Traditionally, educators are taught the thirteen disability categories (see Table 4.1) and hold a basic broad understanding of those disabilities. However, student needs can vary greatly within the same category. Universal design is key to supporting this variability because it asks educators to preplan for differences and remove barriers on the front end, making further differentiation for students with intensive needs more feasible.

Consider the following example: Remember Darryl (see Figure 2.1)? He has attention deficit hyperactivity disorder (ADHD). His ADHD manifests in fidgetiness, inability to attend for long periods of time, and sensory-seeking behavior (he wants to touch everything). Darryl could benefit from sensory breaks,

TABLE 4.1 Thirteen Disability Categories

Disability Category	Description
Autism	A developmental disability significantly affecting verbal and nonverbal communication and social interaction, generally evident before age three.
Deaf-Blindness	Simultaneous hearing and visual impairments that cause severe communication and other developmental and educational needs.
Deafness	A hearing impairment so severe that a child is impaired in processing linguistic information through hearing, with or without amplification.
Emotional Disturbance	A condition exhibiting one or more characteristics over a long period of time, to a marked degree, that adversely affects educational performance.
Hearing Impairment	An impairment in hearing, whether permanent or fluctuating, that adversely affects a child's educational performance.
Intellectual Disability	Significantly subaverage general intellectual functioning, existing concurrently with deficits in adaptive behavior, manifested during the developmental period.
Multiple Disabilities	Concomitant impairments that cause such severe educational needs that they cannot be accommodated in special education programs solely for one of the impairments.
Orthopedic Impairment	A severe orthopedic impairment that adversely affects a child's educational performance. The term includes impairments caused by congenital anomaly or disease.
Other Health Impairment	Having limited strength, vitality, or alertness, including a heightened alertness to environmental stimuli, that results in limited alertness with respect to the educational environment.
Specific Learning Disability	A disorder in one or more of the basic psychological processes involved in understanding or in using language, spoken or written, that may manifest in the imperfect ability to listen, think, speak, read, write, spell, or do mathematical calculations.
Speech or Language Impairment	A communication disorder, such as stuttering, impaired articulation, a language impairment, or a voice impairment, that adversely affects a child's educational performance.
Traumatic Brain Injury	An acquired injury to the brain caused by an external physical force, resulting in total or partial functional disability or psychosocial impairment, or both, that adversely affects educational performance.

Source: Individuals with Disabilities Education Act (2004).

Learner Profiles

Shawn
- Resilient and motivated learner
- Has dyslexia (struggles with spelling and reading fluency)
- Experiences low mood, anger, and defensiveness
- Thrives in a positive and supportive environment

Isaiah
- Strong long-term memory and motivated to learn
- Requires structure, routines, and positive reinforcement
- Has Autism (uneven cognitive skills, stimming, and repetitive behaviors)
- Lagging skills in emotional regulation (managing frustration)

Darryl
- Highly motivated, independent worker who grasps complex concepts well
- Proficient in reading, math, and science
- Has ADD (fidgets and seeks touch stimulation)
- Resilient and collaborative learner

FIGURE 2.1 Learner Profiles for Tailored Instruction. This figure presents profiles of three diverse learners—Shawn, Isaiah, and Darryl—highlighting their strengths, challenges, and specific needs.

chunked tasks, frequent breaks, and flexible seating. Those strategies would also support a student with autism and a student with emotional disabilities. Integrating them into class-wide and school-wide systems increases access and engagement for a wider range of students, allowing the teacher to focus on targeted differentiation for more complex needs.

Supporting students like Darryl requires teachers to understand learner variability and how to universally design lessons with those characteristics and strategies in mind. They must also understand the domains of a learner's system (e.g., *cognitive, emotional, behavioral,* and *academic*), what it looks like when that system is or is not working well, and appropriate supportive strategies. You were introduced to these domains in Chapter 2 (see Table 2.6). In the "Appendix" of this book is a tool, *The Learner Variability Toolkit*, which outlines all of the domains of learning, subdomains, indicators, and supporting strategies. Leaders should leverage this tool as a resource for building educator understanding of learner variability. This tool can be used during coaching and planning meetings to identify targeted strategies aligned with student learner profiles. Integrating the use of the toolkit into planning meetings is a sustainable strategy for building teacher expertise. Table 4.2 provides a snapshot of one element of the toolkit.

Attention

TABLE 4.2 Snapshot of Learner Variability Toolkit—Attention Domain

<u>Subdomain:</u> Mental Energy

<u>Description:</u> Manages the brain's energy supply for information processing and behavior regulation. Individuals with ineffective mental energy control may experience mental fatigue when trying to concentrate, hindering optimal learning and behavior. This system comprises four controls: *alertness* for effective information processing, *sleep and arousal balance* for daytime alertness, *mental effort* to initiate and sustain tasks, and *performance consistency* to ensure a reliable energy flow. Inconsistencies in this control can lead to unpredictable work output and behavior.

Indicators of Need	*Strategies to Support*
♦ has trouble initiating and sticking with tasks ♦ does not seem alert when reading or listening ♦ appears excessively fatigued when working ♦ alertness and energy level fluctuate ♦ fidgets and seeks physical stimulation to stay vigilant ♦ has trouble falling asleep (despite having a calming bedtime routine), staying asleep, and waking	♦ Vary instructional modalities to keep students engaged and alert ♦ Allow movement during work, like standing at desks or using fidgets ♦ Incorporate purposeful breaks in your lessons ♦ Use a segmented writing process for complex tasks ♦ Ensure task stages are brief and focused ♦ Allow for abbreviated writing assignments ♦ Pair students to support each other's alertness and engagement ♦ Vary instructional modalities to keep students engaged and alert

Essential Knowledge for Inclusive School Design

The essential knowledge educators need to design inclusive academic, behavioral, and data systems is detailed within the core practices outlined in each chapter. Table 4.3 summarizes this essential knowledge. To measure your learning growth, use the checklist in Table 4.3 to assess your understanding before and after reading about each principle. This will help you track your progress and comprehension of the key concepts.

TABLE 4.3 Essential Knowledge for Inclusive School Design

Topic	Principle	Essential Knowledge Use the blank rows as a checklist to mark what you know now and your new learnings after reading this book. (Rating Scale 1 = Novice, 2 = Emerging, 3 = Expert)	Pretest	Posttest
Inclusive Practices	Anti-Ableist Program Design	Designing academic and behavioral policies, procedures, and practices that meet the needs of exceptional learners.		
		Creating an environment that promotes belonging for exceptional learners.		
		How to effectively align resources (human capital, use of time, and financial) to drive the success of exceptional learners.		
Data Analysis	Data Urgency	Collecting and analyzing student performance data during and after instruction to identify learning gaps.		
		Progress monitoring on grade-level instruction and interventions.		
		Using data to design scaffolds, inform small group instruction and design interventions.		
Classroom Management	Person-First Culture	Designing classroom routines and procedures that support learner variability.		
		Creating a respectful, safe, and supportive classroom environment.		
Behavior Support	Person-First Culture	Effective strategies to build social, behavioral, and emotional skills.		
		Functions of behavior and appropriate interventions.		
		Using positive reinforcement and proactive behavior management strategies.		
Academic Content Knowledge	Student-Centered Instruction	Academic content knowledge to support diverse learners effectively.		
		Designing accessible grade-level instruction to support diverse learner types.		

High Leverage Practices	Student-Centered Instruction	Evidence-based instructional strategies that have a high impact on student learning. Special education high leverage practices tailored to individual student needs.
Universal Design	Student-Centered Instruction	Incorporating multiple means of representation, engagement, and expression in lesson plans. Planning and executing scaffolding strategies to support diverse learners. Planning to support learner variability.
Mathematics Instruction	Student-Centered Instruction	High leverage practices specific to math instruction. Characteristics of students with math difficulties and implementing supportive strategies. The CRA (Concrete-Representational-Abstract) sequence in teaching math concepts.
Reading Instruction	Student-Centered Instruction	Effective literacy instruction based on the science of reading. Systematic and explicit reading instruction. Explicit comprehension strategy instruction.
Effective Intervention	Student-Centered Instruction	Tiered interventions. Explicit instruction. Progress monitoring to assess intervention effectiveness.

Source: Danielson (2007), Leko et al. (2022), Griffin et al. (2022), Fritz and Harn (2022), McLeskey et al. (2017).

Enabling Conditions to Support Inclusive Professional Learning

The topics outlined in Table 4.3 are comprehensive and may seem overwhelming, but this knowledge is critical to disrupting the status quo and closing the gap for exceptional learners. Leadership teams must have the expertise needed to effectively coach teachers toward this goal, and teachers must possess the knowledge to design instruction and learning environments that meet the needs of every learner. Content knowledge alone is insufficient for general educators, and understanding disability alone is inadequate for special educators. Leaders must create the conditions that empower teachers to effectively wield their knowledge in a sustainable manner while positively impacting student learning.

Leaders can make Inclusive Professional Learning sustainable and feasible by (1) embedding continuous learning opportunities into new or existing structures and tools and (2) reimagining roles and responsibilities to better leverage and strengthen teacher expertise.

Leaders can *embed continuous learning opportunities* as follows:

- Creating predictable meeting structures for collaboration and learning, such as co-planning meetings with an intentional focus on planning for learner variability.
- Scheduling grade-level team meetings where teachers collaboratively problem-solve to support exceptional learners by sharing best practices, identifying challenges, and developing solutions.
- Designing tools that integrate knowledge-building, such as planning templates, meeting protocols, and meeting agendas. For example, a lesson planning protocol that integrates targeted prompts about learner variability (e.g., "How might this lesson create barriers for students with processing difficulties, and what strategies can you leverage to remove or minimize those barriers?").

Leaders can *reimagine roles and responsibilities* as follows:

- Reducing special educator caseload administrative demands to allow a focus on instructional priorities.
- Reimagining traditional instructional coaching roles as inclusion specialists requiring both content expertise and expertise on inclusive practices.
- Assigning special educators to one content area to allow them to build content expertise and meaningfully support students on their caseload.
- Considering hiring general education content experts for the special education role and working to build their expertise in supporting learner variability.
- Creating mentoring and coaching opportunities to build the expertise of novice teachers.
- Focusing on ensuring that teachers supporting students with specific learning needs in literacy and math are provided high-quality instruction by teachers who understand content and learner variability.

By reimagining roles and embedding the understanding of learner variability into school-wide systems and expectations, Inclusive Professional Learning becomes sustainable, systematic, and a part of a school's culture. This approach ensures that all educators, not just special education teachers, gain the knowledge crucial to supporting exceptional learners in an inclusive environment.

Your Role

The call to action for leaders is to:
Empower all educators to understand learner variability.

Understanding learner variability is not just an educational imperative – it's a societal necessity. The failure to appreciate and support difference extends beyond the classroom and affects the fabric of our communities. Students with disabilities, neurodivergent individuals, and other exceptional learners are not just students in a school; they are part of our everyday lives. When they walk into a local coffee shop, dine at a restaurant, or shop at a grocery store, they deserve to be met with empathy and understanding.

Imagine what happens when these students encounter public service workers like police officers and firefighters. Are these interactions met with fear and judgment or respect and support? It is everyone's responsibility—from local business owners to community members and public servants—to understand and respect learner variability. By embracing our shared responsibility, we can create inclusive and supportive communities.

In the school setting, many stakeholders can play a direct role in creating the conditions for educators to build the knowledge and skills needed to create inclusive learning environments. Principals develop and support teachers, superintendents set licensure and training expectations, and funders and policymakers can create incentives in this area. This is a collective effort.

Use Table 4.4 to identify how you can partner in answering the call to action for *Inclusive Professional Learning*.

TABLE 4.4 Stakeholder Role—Inclusive Professional Learning

Stakeholder Role	Support Inclusive Professional Learning
School Leader (Principal, Executive Director, Assistant Principal, etc.)	Embed continuous professional learning opportunities into existing structures, focusing on learner variability and inclusive practices.
Principal Managers and District Leaders	Set a vision for inclusivity, align district-wide expectations to this vision, allocate resources for professional development on learner variability.
Funders	Prioritize funding for professional development initiatives that include training on learner variability and inclusive teaching practices.
School Support Organizations	Design all programs and initiatives to include components that train and support educators in understanding and addressing learner variability.
Policymakers	Mandate professional development practices that include training on learner variability and creating policies or incentives that promote inclusive education for exceptional learners.
Families and Caregivers	Educate themselves about learner variability and participating in school-based training or workshops to model and encourage inclusive attitudes and behaviors.

In the next chapter, you will dive into the systems, practices, and protocols that drive student and adult behavior—school culture, applying the values introduced in the last chapter. This exploration will highlight how inclusive values should drive student and adult behavior, setting the tone for the overall culture of our schools.

Action Planning

Complete the prompts in the space below or use the action planning template (see "Appendix") to outline your next steps for answering this chapter's call to action.

Planning Template

Planning Task	Notes
Final Reflection *Which stakeholder role do you hold and what will you do to commit to the call to action?*	
Goal *Craft one goal aligned with the content of this chapter.*	
Resources *What resources are needed to meet this goal? Consider human capital, scheduling, and finances.*	

Bibliography

Billingsley, B., DeMatthews, D., Raab, R.R., & James, L. (2022). Principal actions in effective inclusive schools: a review of elementary case studies. In J. McLeskey, N. L. Waldron, F. Spooner, & B. Algozzine (Eds.), *Handbook of effective inclusive elementary schools* (2nd ed., pp. 16–42). Routledge.

Connor, D. (2014). Social justice in education for students with disabilities. In *The SAGE Handbook of Special Education: Two* Volume Set (2nd ed., Vol. 2, pp. 111–128). SAGE Publications Ltd, https://doi.org/10.4135/9781446282236

Danielson, C. (2007). *Enhancing Professional Practice: A Framework for Teaching* (2nd ed.). Alexandria, VA: Association for Supervision and Curriculum Development.

DeMatthews, D., Billingsley, B., McLeskey, J., & Cowart Moss, S. (2023). Inclusive principal leadership: Moving toward inclusive and high-achieving schools for students with disabilities (Document No. IC-8b). University of Florida, Collaboration for Effective Educator Development, Accountability, and Reform Center website: http://ceedar.education.ufl.edu/tools/innovation-configurations/

Fritz, R., & Harn, B. (2022). Effective literacy instruction in inclusive schools. In J. McLeskey, N. L. Waldron, F. Spooner, & B. Algozzine (Eds.), *Handbook of effective inclusive elementary schools* (2nd ed., pp. 199–220). Routledge.

Griffin, C., Kwon, J. B., Apraiz, K., & Wong, L.N. (2022). Creating opportunities for struggling mathematics learners in inclusive schools. In J. McLeskey, N. L. Waldron, F. Spooner, & B. Algozzine (Eds.), *Handbook of effective inclusive elementary schools* (2nd ed., pp. 221–244). Routledge.

Individuals with Disabilities Education Act, 20 U.S.C. § 1400 (2004).

Leko, M., Roberts, C., Zepp, L., Chandrashekhar, S., & Forsberg, M. (2022). The role of professional development in inclusive schools. In J. McLeskey, N. L. Waldron, F. Spooner, & B. Algozzine (Eds.), *Handbook of effective inclusive elementary schools* (2nd ed., pp. 16–42). Routledge.

McLeskey, J., Barringer, M.D., Billingsley, B., Brownell, M., Jackson, D., Kennedy, M., & Ziegler, D. (2017). *High-leverage practices in special education*. Arlington, VA: Council for Exceptional Children & CEEDAR Center.

Part 2
The Big Three Systems

5

Principle 3

Person-First Culture

The call to action for leaders is to:
Reframe disciple systems as social-emotional support systems

Old Thinking: Discipline and behavior systems should ensure students abide by school rules and maintain order.
New Thinking: Behavior systems are social-emotional support systems designed to promote belonging and well-being and build social skills.

In This Section

Leaders are responsible for cultivating a learning environment that promotes well-being and student success—a positive school culture. A culture is defined by the beliefs, values, and expectations that drive how students, staff, and the broader community interact. Central to a school's culture are systems for behavior, safety, and well-being, which represent areas of growing concern for educators and caregivers across the country. Specific concerns relate to the lingering effects of the COVID-19 pandemic on student mental health (U.S. Department of Education, 2024), the impact of social media, and the ever-present challenge of supporting students with diagnosed behavioral needs. These challenges signal a need for leaders to prioritize a responsive and supportive approach, one that inclusive education advocates have championed for years.

In this section, leaders will explore how to transform traditional behavior and discipline systems so they create a welcoming and affirming environment that fosters safety, belonging, and well-being for all students, especially exceptional learners.

The call to action to leaders is to:

Reframe discipline systems as social-emotional support systems.

CHAPTER CONTENTS

- Student Story
- The Three Problems: Discipline Systems
- School Example—Van Ness Elementary School
- Why Schools Need to Transform Their Approach to Discipline
- Core Practices
- Your Equity Skills
- Tips for Parents
- Your Role
- Action Planning

Reflecting on the *Three Problems* in Discipline Systems

Are your discipline and classroom management systems inclusive? To be inclusive, they must promote belonging and positive social, emotional, or behavioral outcomes for your exceptional learners. "Belonging is experienced when students are present, invited, welcomed, known, accepted, involved, supported, heard, befriended, and needed" (Carter and Biggs, 2021). In Chapter 1, we explored three problems that inhibit educators' ability to drive these outcomes and perpetuate the status quo for exceptional learners: the *Ownership Problem*, the *Design Problem*, and the *Knowledge Problem*. Let's start our exploration of our discipline and management systems by considering them through the lens of these problems.

> **THE THREE PROBLEMS IN DISCIPLINE**
>
> *Reflect*: Review Table 5.1. Do these problems manifest in your discipline systems? If so, why?

What would you say if someone asked you if your discipline systems were inclusive? If not, why? Improvement requires continuous reflection and evaluation of "why." Throughout this chapter, we will explore how to build inclusive discipline systems and revisit this question at the end.

This is the last time we'll use the terminology "discipline" or "behavior" systems. I am intentionally reframing those terms

TABLE 5.1 The Three Problems-Discipline Systems

Problem	Common Examples in "Discipline Systems"
The Ownership Problem *Are the right individuals accountable for this challenge?*	♦ Special education leaders handle students with behavioral needs exclusively. ♦ General educators refer behavior challenges to special educators instead of addressing them. ♦ Behavioral issues are seen as solely a special education responsibility.
The Design Problem *Does the design of the learning environment promote belonging and social-emotional well-being for exceptional learners?*	♦ Schools use one-size-fits-all discipline policies that ignore individual student needs. ♦ Classrooms have rigid behavior expectations without flexibility for social-emotional needs. ♦ Discipline systems rely on punitive measures.
The Knowledge Problem *Do all educators understand effective practice in this area?*	♦ Educators lack professional development and coaching on addressing the root causes of behavior. ♦ Data-driven approaches to monitor and adjust behavioral interventions are underused.

as "social-emotional support systems." This shift highlights our focus on building social-emotional skills, enhancing student engagement, and promoting overall well-being. Reframing discipline systems as social-emotional support systems asks leaders to move away from the prevailing approach of controlling student behavior through reactive and punitive means helping to mitigate the adverse and disproportionate outcomes for commonly marginalized students and effectively support learner variability.

Let's consider this new approach through the eyes of a student. Read the story about Michael and reflect on how a shift in thinking or approach could have impacted his experience.

Student Story—Michael

PROVOKING QUESTION: What if we reframed discipline and behavior challenges as an opportunity to empathize and innovate instead of viewing the student as a problem?

This story is not a fairy tale with a happy ending but a cautionary tale of what happens when there is a mismatch between the design of a school's system and a student's needs. I can't talk about student behavior without talking about my former student Michael (name changed for privacy), a middle schooler with a diagnosed behavioral disability. I was the interim principal and had only been at the school for a few months, but in that short time, I saw firsthand how Michael struggled and how his teachers struggled to support him. He demonstrated many common characteristics of a student diagnosed with emotional disturbance; he eloped from the classroom, was verbally aggressive toward peers and adults, and was impulsive. After an incident where Michael stole school property, he was suspended after the special education team determined his behavior was not the manifestation of his disability. Following this decision, I received a call from my supervisor. "Toni, this was your opportunity to get rid of Michael; he has been terrorizing the school all year; you need to expel him." Feeling pressure from my supervisor and the staff, I expelled him. A year later, Michael was on the national list of missing and exploited children.

Whenever I tell Michael's story, I wonder what more I could have done to support him. Did he have high-quality behavior supports? Was he receiving skill development on lagging social, emotional, and behavioral skills? Did his team understand the root cause of his behavior? The list goes on. The answer to most of those questions is *that we could have done more; what we did* was *insufficient*. I will forever live with the question, "If these supports were in place for Michael, would his story be different?"

While it continues to be true that schools are struggling to appropriately support students with identified behavioral needs (Hott et al., 2021), you do not have to end up with a "Michael" as a part of your leadership story; you can decide now that your students will not become part of these statistics. You can now decide to commit to creating strong support systems for students' social, emotional, and behavioral needs. You can decide now that when faced with a student like Michael, you will reflect on whether there is something wrong with the system instead of thinking there is something wrong with the student.

> **A CHALLENGING STUDENT**
>
> *Reflect*: *Think about a student with social, emotional, or behavioral challenges whose needs have not been met. Describe the student's challenges. After reading this chapter, you will answer the question, "What changes are needed to support this student's success?"*

Why Schools Need to Transform Their Approach to Discipline

You're defiant!" "That's disrespectful!" "She has an attitude problem!" These are common teacher reactions to challenging student behavior. For years, student engagement and behavior have been an ever-present pain point for educators, especially regarding students with emotional, behavioral, or social concerns. Negative beliefs and overly harsh policies and practices are causing disproportionately poor outcomes for students with disabilities, especially students of color with disabilities. Addressing these pain points is possible but will require a shift toward positive preventative and student-centered support systems—a *Person-First Culture*—that promotes safety, emotional well-being, and belonging.

A school's culture encompasses the routines, policies, protocols, and practices that influence individual behavior, group behavior, and relationships. Traditionally, these systems are known as management systems or discipline systems. The design of these systems can be approached in two ways—through proactive, positive, evidence-backed methods such as restorative practices and positive behavior supports that foster holistic development—or through punitive and exclusionary methods detrimental to student well-being, such as suspensions, expulsions, demerit systems, exclusion, and restraints (McIntosh et al., 2021; Simonsen & George, 2022; Wriston & Duchesneau, 2023). The first approach leads to stronger overall student outcomes, yet schools continue to face challenges in achieving these goals. Here are some potential causes:

- Leaders fall victim to implementing isolated initiatives without a cohesive strategy focused on the overarching goals.
- Misalignment between educator mindsets and what the research says about behavior.
- Educators leave preparation programs without coursework on effective behavior support.
- Expertise in supporting students with behavior challenges is siloed.
- Leadership development does not include a focus on effective behavior support. Of the top five education administration programs (U.S. News & World Report, 2024), not one requires coursework on inclusive education or includes content on effective behavior support).
- Management systems are reactive (Fenning et al., 2004).

The great news is that the buck stops here! While these challenges may seem daunting, after reading this chapter, you will understand the characteristics of robust social-emotional support systems and be well on your way to knowing how to create a supportive and nurturing school environment where students with and without disabilities can thrive socially, emotionally, and academically.

When it comes to supporting student behavioral, social, and emotional skills, commonly referenced frameworks are Positive Behavior Interventions and Supports (PBIS), Restorative Practices, Social-Emotional Learning, and Culturally Responsive Teaching. Supporting students in these areas cannot be effectively addressed by a single initiative. These initiatives encompass mindsets, practices, and policies strategically designed to promote well-being. Leaders must build their knowledge and skills around the specific practices and sage them to support their goals.

Consider the following graphic:

Belonging (acceptance by and connection to a community) and social-emotional well-being

REQUIRES

Students to be able to:	Systems that include:	Educators that know
• Interact with peers and adults • Resolve conflict • Manage feelings • Exhibit empathy • Exhibit self-esteem	• Restorative and relationship-focused discipline policies • Positive behavior interventions and supports • Practices and routines that support student holistic development • Coaching around effective behavior support	• The science of behavior • How to respond during student stress cycle • How environment impacts behavior

FIGURE 5.1 Essential Components of Effective Behavior Support Systems. This figure outlines the interconnected roles of students, systems, and educators in fostering positive behavioral outcomes. It emphasizes the importance of relationship-focused discipline, structured routines, and educator expertise in behavior science and stress responses. (United States Government Accountability Office, 2018; Wriston & Duchesneau, 2023).

The three requirements depicted in the graphic align with those commonly used frameworks. Recent research (Leverson et al., 2021) identifies how these frameworks can be integrated to promote a holistic student-centered approach and urges leaders to prioritize practices, not programs (Simonsen & George, 2022). The Center for Positive Behavior Support, a leading organization in the field, has developed a guide integrating two of those frameworks—one focused on harnessing students' diverse cultures and experiences and another focused on proactive and positive behavior systems—into a comprehensive strategy (Leverson et al., 2021). This emphasizes the significance of an integrated approach in comprehending these frameworks, enabling school leaders to implement them more effectively. The practices outlined in this chapter integrate the elements of those frameworks into a digestible set of actions leaders can take to achieve the goals outlined in Figure 5.1.

Principle In Action: Van Ness Elementary School

What does this look like in practice? Let me introduce you to Van Ness Elementary School, a K–5 school in Washington, DC, which has garnered national attention for its work in developing the *Whole Child Framework*. Van Ness's work has been highlighted in case studies, conferences, and several articles. In a 2022 case study, artfully describes what a peek into a Van Ness classroom looks like (Liebtag, 2021). You will find a welcoming atmosphere focused on supporting student social-emotional development. Teachers meet students with positive daily greetings, the classroom walls reflect their students and their classroom community, and students have reflective spaces to take breaks and learn to manage challenging emotions. The school community is committed to both learning and holistic student development and well-being. Their discipline policies align with these goals, and their day-to-day routines support their goals of investing in student social, emotional, and behavioral development as a prerequisite to their cognitive development (Whole Child Model, n.d.). They include 1:1 student check-ins, mindfulness activities, explicit teaching of self-regulation skills (for both adults and students), and procedures to support relationship-building and conflict management. Their approach has resulted in student, family, and staff satisfaction and strong academic performance in early childhood classrooms (Liebtag, 2021).

Understanding Learner Variability in Behavior

When students face social, emotional, or behavioral challenges, these difficulties typically stem from lagging skills in one or more areas. Ross Greene, the author of *The Explosive Child*, categorizes these skills into four main areas, as outlined in Table 5.2. Understanding these challenges as skill deficits provides a useful framework for leaders to create social-emotional support systems that proactively integrate support for students with needs in these areas.

The term "emotional disturbance" (ED) is the technical term defined by the Individuals with Disabilities Education Act (IDEA). It is the most widely recognized classification for students with diagnosed social, emotional, and behavioral challenges (IDEA, 2004). However, behavioral challenges can occur

TABLE 5.2 Behavioral Lagging Skills and Supporting Strategies

Lagging Skill	Examples	Supportive Strategies
Executive Function	Limited working memory, poor impulse control, black-and-white thinking, difficulty deviating from rules or routine	Use visual schedules, break tasks into smaller steps, and teach organizational skills
Emotion Regulation	Emotional reactivity, chronic irritability, and/or anxiety	Implement calming techniques, teach coping strategies, and provide a safe space
Language	Limited expressive language, difficulty with language processing	Use visual supports, simplify language, provide speech and language therapy
Social Skills	Poor perception of social cues, difficulty starting conversations	Teach social skills explicitly, use role-playing, provide peer interaction opportunities

Source: Greene (2014b).

TABLE 5.3 Common Disability Categories and Potential Behavior Challenges

Disability Category	Potential Behavior Challenges
Autism	Repetitive behaviors, difficulty with social interactions, resistance to change, sensory sensitivities
ED	Aggression, anxiety, depression, mood swings, defiance
ADHD	Impulsivity, hyperactivity, inattentiveness, difficulty following instructions
Learning Disabilities	Frustration, avoidance of academic tasks, low self-esteem, inattentiveness
Intellectual Disabilities	Difficulty understanding social cues, frustration, aggression, self-injurious behaviors

Source: Individual with Disabilities Education Act (2004).

across various disability types, including autism, ADHD, learning disabilities, and intellectual disabilities. Each of these disabilities can present unique behavioral challenges due to specific skill deficits or unmet needs. Table 5.3 outlines common disability categories and the potential behavior challenges students with these classifications may exhibit.

Educators must focus on understanding targeted behavior through the following process: identifying the root cause, recognizing the lagging skill, understanding the communication of need, and determining the support needed. Leaders must also understand learner variability in behavior to effectively coach and provide feedback to teachers as they strive to effectively support student needs. An in-depth examination of specific behavior challenges is beyond the scope of this book. Here are a few informative resources that I have leveraged in my own work:

- *The Explosive Child* by Ross Greene
- *Conscious Discipline* by Becky Bailey
- *The Behavior Code* by Jessica Minahan and Nancy Rappaport

Person-First Culture: Core Practices

Let us now explore the characteristics of a *Person-First Culture* as outlined in the Blueprint for Inclusive School-Wide Systems

TABLE 5.4 Core Practices: Person-First Culture

Core Practice	Description
Supportive Classroom Management Systems	Rules, routines, procedures, and rituals should promote belonging, safety, engagement, and well-being.
Strategic Relationship-Building	Systems build strong, authentic relationships between educators and students to promote a positive learning environment.
Social-Emotional Skill Development	Systems explicitly teach students to develop self-awareness, self-regulation, social skills, and responsible decision-making.
Aligned and Explicit Behavior Intervention	Evidence-based behavior intervention strategies aligned with student needs.

(BLISS). As explained in the introduction, the BLISS Framework is an evidence and research-based framework designed to intentionally integrate the elements of relevant equity frameworks (e.g., PBIS, UDL, Restorative Practices, MTSS) in a way that is digestible and usable for leaders, allowing them to focus on specific practices and less on the *title* of an initiative. My goal is for you to view these broader frameworks as a set of connected practices defining how you should approach school-wide systems design.

The BLISS Framework outlines six core practices that define a Person-First Culture.

Core Practice 1: Supportive Classroom Management Systems

Description: Rules, routines, procedures, and rituals should promote belonging, safety, engagement, and well-being.

Classroom management systems encompass the rules, routines, procedures, and rituals that drive student behavior. Supportive management systems promote belonging, safety, engagement, and well-being. They are preventive, positive, and respectful, intentionally supporting student differences. Research has consistently shown that students with emotional, behavioral, and social challenges benefit from an evidence-based continuum of supports grounded in a supportive approach, which, when effectively implemented, promotes positive relationships and well-being while reducing discipline disparities (Fenning & Jenkins, 2018; Simonsen & George, 2022).

Indicator: Management Systems Are Supportive of Student Differences

Teachers must know and understand student individual differences to develop classroom rules, procedures, and routines that do not adversely impact any group or individual. They should also understand how their own experiences and culture influence their expectations around behavior (Leverson et al., 2021). What is considered "normal" or "appropriate" is not the same for all individuals and can differ based on a student's home environment, geographical location, or family values and rituals. By engaging families and developing a broader understanding of the background of their students, educators can develop systems that are reflective and responsive to student individuality (2021).

Indicator: Supportive, Preventive, and Positive Discipline Policies

Strong systems for student discipline and behavior (social-emotional support systems) should be supported by written policies designed to be supportive, preventive, and positive (cite PBIS, Fenning et al. Leverson et al., 2021). Expectations should be modeled, explicitly taught, and implemented consistently. Students with social, emotional, or behavioral challenges especially benefit from explicit expectations that respect student disability, culture, or other individual needs.

The state of Illinois is leading the way in creating person-first systems for discipline and behavior through its Transforming School Discipline Collaborative (a membership of state legislators, nonprofits, higher education partners, administrators, and others). The Collaborative started as a state-wide initiative focused on reducing exclusionary discipline and the disproportionate impact of exclusionary policies on marginalized student groups, including students with disabilities (Transforming School Discipline Collaborative, n.d.). They have developed school guidance and tools, including a model disciplinary code. This code is an example of strategically integrating Positive Behavior Support (PBS) and Restorative Practices, which helps to support clarity and ease of implementation for leaders.

Some key components of the code are as follows:

- Discipline is not used as a punishment but instead as an opportunity for support, learning, growth, and community-building
- Families and other stakeholders collaborated to support policy development
- Details specific preventative measures and differentiated interventions (e.g., referrals for mental health support, classroom-based interventions, mediation)
- Focus on teaching appropriate behaviors
- Prioritization of repairing and restoring harmed relationships
- Includes expectations and guidelines for professional development, ensuring staff have the necessary skills to implement policy (e.g., training on trauma, implicit bias, positive behavior intervention, de-escalation, restorative practices, effective classroom management, culturally responsive discipline)
- Reengagement plan (if deemed appropriate) outlining a process for student re-entry and details strategies to prevent recurring behavior and targeted interventions to support future success for the student
- Outlines exclusionary discipline as a last resort, details when it may be appropriate, and alternative education options if exclusionary discipline is implemented

---

TRADITIONAL VS. SUPPORTIVE MANAGEMENT SYSTEMS

Reflect: *Review details about the Illinois code and answer one of the following questions:*
1. *How does this differ from traditional policies and approaches to student discipline and behavior?*
2. *What makes this person-first and student-centered?*
3. *What inspires you about their approach?*

Indicator: Explicit Expectations, Reinforcements, and Consequences

Rules and expectations for behavior must be modeled, explicitly taught, and supported by consistent routines. Teachers who develop routines and expectations in partnership with students are more likely to create systems that are responsive to student identity and learner variability. Rules should be developmentally appropriate, not single out students, or applied in a way that conflicts with a student's disability.

Imagine that you had attention deficit order and had challenges with processing information and sustaining attention. How many common classroom expectations conflict with needs in these areas? I often remind leaders that we, as adults, are guilty of setting expectations for students that we do not have of ourselves. I have visited schools where early elementary students are expected to sit attentively with their feet under their desks and their hands folded neatly as the teacher instructs, yet in a professional development session with leaders of those schools, leaders are texting, fidgeting, doodling, and engaging in other self-regulatory behaviors necessary to sustain their own attention.

While setting person-first expectations and routines is critical, understanding effective reinforcement and consequences as essential to a supportive management system is equally important. Despite a growing misconception among educators that proactive and positive behavior systems imply immunity from consequences, **students need consequences**. Consequences are essential tools for teaching prosocial behavior and for building and strengthening social-emotional skills (Campbell, 1999; Minahan & Rappaport, 2012; Kelly & Pohl, 2018). Leaders should create a graduated system of reinforcement and consequences before employing negative consequences (e.g., reminders, redirection, reinforcement, and use of nonverbal cues). Effective consequences are

- natural and logical responses to student behavior,
- applied in a way that educates the student,
- applied alongside positive consequences,
- logical to the undesirable behavior,

- applied immediately, and
- considerate of a student's dignity (firm but anger-free).

Positive reinforcement is also a critical component of an effective social-emotional support system. It increases the likelihood of desired behavior. Reinforcers or rewards should motivate the student and do not have to be tangible or cost money. They may include praise, free time, or preferred activities. Positive reinforcements are especially critical for students with diagnosed behavioral concerns who need a combination of explicit instruction of desired behaviors, positive reinforcements, and appropriate consequences.

> **TRADITIONAL VS SUPPORTIVE MANAGEMENT SYSTEMS**
>
> *Reflect*: *Review the indicators and warning signs of supportive classroom management in Table 5.5. Based on your experience or context, what are your strengths and opportunities for growth?*

Core Practice 2: Strategic Relationship-Building

Description: Systems build strong, authentic relationships between educators and students to promote a positive learning environment.

"I'm not here to be their friend!" This is a common sentiment heard from teachers. Friendship is not and should not be the goal. The goal is a positive teacher-student relationship and is critical to student success and well-being; when students believe teachers care about them, they are more likely to meet expectations. Having taught students diagnosed with emotional and behavioral disabilities, I saw firsthand that my success in getting them to engage, follow directions, and maintain focus was solely the result of high expectations and a positive relationship.

Chris Emdin, a prominent educator and author, has extensively discussed the significance of relationships in school. Emdin posits that teaching and learning do not occur in a vacuum but are human experiences rooted in relationships (Emdin, 2016), the cornerstone of education. He asserts that students are unlikely

TABLE 5.5 Supportive Classroom Management

PERSON-FIRST CULTURE: Supportive Classroom Management	
Indicators	Warning Signs
♦ Teachers set clearly defined expectations and routines for classroom procedures (student discourse, classwork, organization) ♦ Classroom rules are developmentally appropriate and applied in a way that support social-emotional well-being of students and do not single out students ♦ Students with specific learning needs are not expected to exhibit behaviors that conflict with their disability or needs ♦ Teacher cues (verbal and nonverbal) are supportive ♦ Teacher models expected student behavior ♦ Classroom environment promotes belonging across all identity markers and communicates a respect for difference ♦ Teachers recognize their own cultural lens and biases and proactively seek to understand student's cultural backgrounds ♦ Leaders and teachers proactively work to ensure discipline practices do not discriminate against certain students ♦ Teachers view perceived negative student responses and reactions with empathy and understanding	♦ Students lack consistent norms and routines for classroom procedures, leading to potential disorganization and confusion ♦ Classroom rules are not aligned with developmental expectations (see Yardsticks) ♦ Students with attention needs (e.g. fidgety, difficulty with remaining on task, sitting for long periods of time, sustaining focus, managing emotions, shifting focus, getting started, managing time) are expected to exhibit those behaviors and are given consequences for not displaying those behaviors ♦ Corrections are focused solely on compliance with rules ♦ Teacher language and tone are negative or disparaging ♦ Teachers blame students for their behavioral challenges ♦ Teachers respond to student behavioral needs arbitrarily or only by delivering consequences ♦ Consequences are not aligned to student behavior or don't support deterring student behavior ♦ Classroom environment is not representative of the entire school community ♦ Teacher actions demonstrate bias or discrimination toward one or more student groups ♦ Discipline practices adversely impact one student demographic over another

to learn from teachers they do not like or feel connected to. Integrating student cultural identities can support this connection and is especially important for exceptional learners, given the barriers they commonly face in the school setting.

A systematic approach to relationship-building also requires intentionality in hiring and staffing. Relationship-building is strengthened when students have access to staff representative of their own background and culture. Growing research indicates that diversity in the teacher workforce promotes reduced bias and stronger support for diverse student populations (Lewis & Toldson, 2013).

Strategic relationship-building, as defined in *BLISS*, is outlined in Table 5.6.

At Valor Collegiate in Nashville, students and staff participate in a routine called Circle, a systematized routine designed to promote well-being and build relationships. The Circle practice is grounded in Valor's values and is one of the most important elements of their school culture. This is a standardized expectation and consistent routine across the school. Some of the standard parts of this routine include the following:

- **Community Gathering**: Consistently scheduled routine for staff and students to build community
- **Reflection**: The community reflects on relevant topics and shared values to reinforce community commitments and accountability
- **Check-In**: Individuals can share their current mental state and request support if needed
- **Celebration**: Opportunity to recognize community members for their efforts and successes

TABLE 5.6 Strategic Relationship-Building

PERSON-FIRST CULTURE: Supportive Classroom Management	
Indicators	*Warning Signs*
◆ There are clear expectations, routines, and systems that support positive peer:peer and peer:adult relationship-building ◆ Students with specific social-emotional or behavioral needs check-in with a trusted adult at least once per day ◆ Teachers and leaders use authentic affirmation to validate student actions, ideas and contributions, and encourage students to do the same of one another ◆ Students communicate and cooperate with peers and adults in a way that promotes a positive classroom climate	◆ Evidence of teacher-student relationships is inconsistent or nonexistent ◆ Teachers are seen as authoritarian figures ◆ Students struggle with peer-to-peer or peer-to-adult relationships ◆ Student communication with adults or other peers is negative, authoritarian in nature, or nonexistent ◆ Students with social-emotional or behavioral needs can't identify a trusted adult

If you were to peek into the window of a Valor Circle, you would see students being led by a staff member. Over time, students take ownership of leading the Circle, helping to build social-emotional skills. You will also see a staff-only version of Circle, promoting relationships among the staff. This has led to a positive school culture where students and staff feel like a part of a welcoming and affirming community. They feel a sense of belonging.

MULTIMEDIA REFLECTION: Choose one of the following activities to learn more about how some schools approach strategic relationship-building. *Answer*: What inspires you about this example?

Listen to Episode 5 of the *School Disrupted Podcast*: "Stories to Learn From, A Student-Centered Model at Statesman."

Watch a video to see Valor's Circle in action.

FIGURE 5.2 QR Code for Extended Learning Materials. Scan this code to explore additional materials and tools designed to enhance understanding of the chapter's key concepts.

FIGURE 5.3 QR Code for Additional Chapter Resources. Scan this code to access curated digital resources that expand on key concepts covered in this section.

Core Practice 3: Social and Emotional Skill Development

Description: Systems explicitly teach students to develop self-awareness, self-regulation, social skills, and responsible decision-making.

Success in school requires students to have the ability to make constructive choices about personal behavior and social interactions, evaluate the consequences of their actions, communicate and cooperate with others, and manage thoughts and emotions. Educators must intentionally work to hone these skills, particularly for students with known social, emotional, and behavioral needs (Simonsen & George, 2022).

Numerous resources and curricula are available to schools seeking to integrate social and emotional skill development into their academic programs and school schedules. *What Works Clearinghouse*, a resource funded by the Department of Education, provides educators with evidence-based recommended resources that can be leveraged to support students in this area. Table 5.7

TABLE 5.7 Social-Emotional Skill Development

PERSON-FIRST CULTURE: Social and Emotional Skill Development	
Indicators	*Warning Signs*
♦ Students make constructive choices about personal behavior and social interactions, evaluate consequences of various actions, and consider the well-being of themselves and others ♦ Students understand others' perspectives ♦ Students can empathize with others ♦ Students understand social and ethical norms for behavior ♦ Students are self-aware, they recognize their own emotions, thoughts, and values and how they influence behavior ♦ Students can self-regulate their thoughts, emotions, and behaviors in different situations, they are able to identify their current state of emotional regulation ♦ Students identify the connection between their physiological state and their emotional reaction ♦ Students effectively manage stress, and control impulses ♦ Students are able to motivate themselves, set and work toward personal and academic goals ♦ Students can communicate clearly, listen well, cooperate with others, resist inappropriate social pressure, negotiate conflict constructively, and seek and offer help when needed	♦ Students make poor decisions in academic and social settings, they act without thinking about consequences ♦ Students do not consider the impact of their behavior on others ♦ Students struggle to or cannot explain the impact of their emotions on their behaviors ♦ Students cannot explain how thoughts and actions align ♦ Students do not recognize that conflicts often arise due to differing values ♦ Students are not self-aware, they act solely out of self-interest with no thought to other perspectives and do not demonstrate empathy through their words or actions ♦ Students struggle to demonstrate appropriate behavior in the school setting ♦ During times of stress, students struggle to control/regulate their emotions and impulses ♦ Students struggle with social situations ♦ Students who demonstrate behavioral concerns receive frequent disciplinary action (e.g. demerits, referrals, suspension) ♦ Students with social-emotional needs are frequently referred for more restrictive services ♦ Skills taught are not transferred across settings

outlines indicators of effective systems for social and emotional skill development.

Van Ness Elementary School in Washington, DC, and Transcend Education worked to develop a strategic approach to supporting social-emotional skill development, the *Whole Child Model*. The model is grounded in the belief that student academic success is connected to their overall well-being. It prioritizes relationship-building, adult and student self-regulation, classroom environment, targeted behavioral interventions, and family engagement. Their approach has led to student, family, and staff satisfaction and is being widely shared across DC and nationally.

Core Practice 4: Aligned and Explicit Behavior Intervention

Description: Evidence-based behavior intervention strategies aligned with student needs.

Sometimes, school-wide and classroom-based supports are insufficient to support students with behavior challenges. Students who are nonresponsive to classroom-based supports and those with diagnosed social, emotional, or behavioral challenges may require targeted interventions, explicit skill development, and other wraparound supports. Typically, when students exhibit challenging behavior, there is an underlying reason or unmet need. Effective educators recognize behavior challenges as a social-emotional need and work to identify the need or root cause.

Our perception of what constitutes challenging behavior must be grounded in a strengths-based, culturally responsive, and bias-free perspective. There is one question educators can ask themselves to check their own potential bias: *"Is my response to this behavior based on personal expectations, my own cultural norms, or my potential discomfort?"* This can help avoid unnecessary and adverse responses to subjectively annoying or offensive behaviors that are not otherwise harmful. There are some common reasons a student may exhibit challenging behavior (Minahan & Rappaport, 2012). Understanding these will strengthen your development of effective policies and procedures and support your teachers' ability to respond effectively.

♦ To escape a task, demand, situation, or person
♦ To obtain a tangible benefit
♦ Sensory stimulation
♦ To gain attention

It is common to be reactive to student behavior challenges. Minahan and Rapaport offer guidance to leaders on how to mitigate this through proactively considering the following in systems design:

♦ How can we plan for students with known challenges by integrating proactive support into classroom systems?
♦ What is our approach to teaching replacement behaviors and undeveloped skills?
♦ How are we systematically reinforcing desired behaviors?
♦ How should we interact with students to prevent behavior challenges?
♦ How should we respond to students exhibiting challenging behavior in a way that both deters and supports them (Minahan & Rappaport, 2012)?

Educators must become adept at identifying what students are trying to accomplish with their behavior and responding accordingly. Students' internal mental and emotional states are constantly changing, and those with social, behavioral, or emotional challenges need support in building the skills needed to appropriately manage challenges when they present. In addition to explicit instruction of desired behaviors, strategies for effective behavior support may include self-management, social skills instruction, relationship management, accountability systems, and counseling (U.S. Department of Education, 2022). This chapter does not delve into every possible intervention for addressing challenging behavior but is designed to build your schema around key aspects of supporting and understanding behavior. Indicators of this core practice are outlined in Table 5.8.

TABLE 5.8 Aligned and Explicit Interventions

PERSON-FIRST CULTURE: Aligned and Explicit Behavior Intervention	
Indicators	Warning Signs
◆ Teachers recognize behavioral challenges as social-emotional needs and work to identify and support root cause (understand likes, dislikes, triggers, strengths, and needs) ◆ Students who are not responsive to universal behavioral supports, or those with identified social-emotional needs, receive evidence-based interventions aligned to their needs ◆ Targeted interventions are based upon a variety of behavioral data (e.g. anecdotal classroom observations, parent reports, behavior checklists) ◆ Behavioral supports are monitored and adjusted as necessary ◆ All adults (paraprofessionals, teacher, school leaders, etc.) are normed on the implementation of behavioral support plans and execute plans with fidelity ◆ Student strengths are leveraged to inform intervention ◆ Students practice and apply skills taught on a daily basis	◆ Students who demonstrate behavioral concerns receive frequent disciplinary action (e.g. demerits, referrals, suspension) ◆ Students with social-emotional needs are frequently referred for more restrictive services ◆ Interventions are uniformly implemented or not implemented at all ◆ Students are assigned to interventions without thought to their existing strengths or areas of need ◆ Skills taught are not transferred across settings

Comprehensive Adult and Student Well-Being Supports

Teachers consistently express concerns about lacking tools to support students with social, emotional, or behavioral needs. There are also concerns about increased behavioral challenges among the broader student population. Addressing this requires a comprehensive and systematic approach to adult and student well-being. We often focus on the need for teachers to learn about and understand the science of behavior and how to support students effectively but do not always consider the impact on teacher well-being.

> ✓ 98,000 students are physically restrained or secluded
> ✓ 92,000 students receive corporal punishment
> ✓ 101,000 students are expelled from
> ✓ 5 million students receive in or out-of-school suspensions

Current research stresses the importance of teacher well-being and mental health as essential to student success and teacher retention and self-efficacy. A 2024 report by RAND found that teachers need access to mental health supports and supportive working environments (RAND, 2024). Some of the supports may include support with administrative tasks and external partnerships to reduce teacher workload and create a positive adult culture (2024). If leaders expect teachers to effectively support students' social, emotional, and behavioral needs, they must be equally intentional about supporting teachers in these areas.

Application: Shawn, Darryl, and Isaiah

Reflect: Which core practice would best support Shawn or Isaiah, and why? How might those core practices be standardized across school-wide routines and procedures?

Learner Profiles

Shawn

- Resilient and motivated learner
- Has dyslexia (struggles with spelling and reading fluency)
- Experiences low mood, anger, and defensiveness
- Thrives in a positive and supportive environment

Isaiah

- Strong long-term memory and motivated to learn
- Requires structure, routines, and positive reinforcement
- Has Autism (uneven cognitive skills, stimming, and repetitive behaviors)
- Lagging skills in emotional regulation (managing frustration)

Darryl

- Highly motivated, independent worker who grasps complex concepts well
- Proficient in reading, math, and science
- Has ADD (fidgets and seeks touch stimulation)
- Resilient and collaborative learner

FIGURE 2.1 Learner Profiles for Tailored Instruction. This figure presents profiles of three diverse learners—Shawn, Isaiah, and Darryl—highlighting their strengths, challenges, and specific needs.

What About 'That' Kid... Their Behavior Is Too Challenging

There are certain students many educators think do not belong in the regular classroom. In some cases, they don't believe they belong in a school setting at all. These students typically have a behavioral need or challenge so significant it interferes with their ability to interact with others, maintain positive peer or adult relationships, or with their own or other's safety. Every educator knows of a student who fits this profile. As a result of a lack of appropriate support, educator skills, and punitive approaches, every year, students are subjected to harsh disciplinary actions likely to lead to negative post-secondary outcomes.

Ross Greene and other researchers on behavior instruct us that challenging students do not lack motivation. They lack skills. Working to build these skills can prevent future problems for these students. In his 2019 article, Greene noted that challenging behaviors present when there is a mismatch between an individual's learner profile and the design of their environment.

The Collaborative and Proactive Solutions model, formerly called *Collaborative Problem-Solving*, is an intentional approach to supporting students with lagging social, emotional, and behavioral skills. This approach has been widely successful for youth in outpatient settings, therapeutic settings, and schools. This approach supports behavior change by focusing on the following:

- Identifying lagging social, emotional, or behavioral skills.
- Identifying the problem causing the behavior.
- Examining how adult expectations might precipitate challenging behavior.
- Determining whether behavior support and response systems prioritize crisis management or crisis prevention.
- Assessing whether systems focus on adult and child problem-solving or compliance with adult directives.
- Ensuring a positive relationship exists between the student and caregiver.
- Ensuring the caregiver's approach is warm and welcoming.

- Intentionally addressing negative emotions and teaching appropriate emotional responses.
- Building adult proficiency in responding to and preventing negative behavior.
- Understanding how the environment contributes to behavior and creating a "user-friendly" environment (Greene & Winkler, 2019; Greene et al., 2006).

You can find more information and tools aligned to Collaborative Problem-Solving and Ross's book *Lost at School* (Greene, 2014a) at www.lostatschool.org.

Supporting students with disability-based behavior challenges is not easy, and its challenges should not be sugarcoated. Inclusive, socially just leaders commit to creating welcoming, safe, and affirming school communities for all students, not just the easy ones. To do so, you must seek to understand disability-based behavior and work to intentionally create policies that are supportive and not discriminatory, oppressive, or exclusionary. A positive approach to behavior can significantly reduce challenging behavior and must accompany any approach to supporting disability-based behavior (U.S. Department of Education, 2022).

Your Equity Skills

In Chapter 1, I introduced you to the *Five Abilities of Equity Literacy* (Gorski & Swalwell, 2023), the five skills leaders should possess to become true equity leaders. As a reminder, we will reflect on these skills in the context of each of the *Big 3 Systems* to strengthen your equity literacy and your ability to create and lead transformative systems for exceptional learners and disrupt inequity when it exists. As Gorski and Swalwell remind us, we must practice using these skills if we are going to be adept at driving equity in our schools (2023).

You have spent time understanding the characteristics of inclusive social-emotional support systems, a *Person-First Culture*. You are now ready to reflect on whether the systems in your school are promoting or preventing equity for your exceptional learners. Let us review the five skills in relation to a Person-First Culture. You will then reflect on each in your context.

Recognize Inequity. The first equity skill a leader must possess is the ability to recognize when inequity exists. In what ways might policies, practices, or protocols be targeting or disproportionately negatively affecting exceptional learners? A precursor to answering these questions is knowing how to effectively support student social, emotional, and behavioral needs, particularly those with diagnosed disabilities in these areas. Leaders must then analyze existing discipline policies at the school and classroom level and the day-to-day classroom practices related to student behavior. For example, are teachers using "color charts" or "red light/green light" behavior monitoring systems that focus on negative reinforcement, seem punitive, or disproportionately impact students whose disability requires increased amounts of positive reinforcement, such as students with autism or oppositional defiance disorder?

Respond to Inequity. Once you've recognized inequity, the obvious next step is to do something about it. The question leaders are to answer now is, How will you react to address the impact of the inequitable practice? If you recognize that policies are incompatible with the needs of students with emotional or behavioral disabilities, how will you respond appropriately?

Redress Inequity. Here, leaders must unpack the potential root causes of existing inequities. This may include mindsets, underrepresented voices, missing perspectives, etc. Here, the inclusive values are relevant, and the absence of one or more of those values could lead to inequity. Redressing inequity may require revamping classroom expectations to incorporate supportive practices such as alternative seating arrangements and positive reinforcements or revising the discipline policy to integrate proactive interventions and reinforcement strategies instead of solely consequences. In addition, teachers are coached on instructional practices that promote engagement, and all staff receive training and support on understanding and effectively responding to challenging behavior. Mindset work is vital here.

Many educators hold the opinion that "those kids are not my problem"; this is where leaders must revisit their school's values and reflect on whether the supporting conditions are in place that ensure teachers have the capacity (knowledge, time, and stamina) and the willingness to do effectively support these students. Remember, "will over skill" is critical.

Cultivate Equity. Here is where leaders shift to proactive action. The goal is to actively develop or revise policies, protocols, practices, and procedures to promote justice and normalize equity for exceptional learners. Leaders should work to build systems and protocols that incorporate an equity lens. During an interview, Kevin Lohela, the principal of an inclusive elementary school, shared that he prioritizes "will over skill" in hiring decisions. He prioritizes hiring staff with a growth mindset and a commitment to inclusivity. I had the opportunity to visit his classrooms numerous times and interview many of his staff who echoed his philosophy and exhibited these values through their team meetings. I observed the Child Study Meeting, a structure used to plan for students with behavior challenges, and heard the team begin the meeting by reflecting on the school's values and committing to how they will live those values in the meeting. Two commitments were "talk like the child's family is in the room" and "behavior can be changed." These are examples of working to cultivate equity.

Sustain Equity. Equity is an ongoing goal and requires consistency and commitment, especially when things get hard, which is often the case when addressing student social-emotional needs. When a student with an emotional disability throws a chair or flips over a desk, what is your default response? Is it, "Get that kid out of here; he doesn't belong," or do you apply an equity lens and ask, "What conditions led to this behavior, and how can I support this student and the teacher?" Sustaining equity requires leaders to have systems for

- ensuring teachers understand student behavior,
- providing teachers respite from stressful incidents,
- proactively supporting student and staff well-being, and
- collaborating with families.

Review Table 5.9 to reflect on your equity abilities within social-emotional support systems. When you finish, you will be ready to review the *call to action* and set your individual goals in the final section of this chapter, "Action Planning."

TABLE 5.9 Equity Skills in a Person-First Culture

Equity Abilities	Reflection Question	Potential Response
Recognize Inequity *Identify how policies, practices, or protocols are negatively affecting exceptional learners*	♦ Do my behavior policies and practices disadvantage students with social, emotional, or behavioral disabilities? ♦ Are there school or classroom expectations based on one group's norms or traditions to the detriment of other groups?	♦ Students with diagnosed behavioral challenges are being disciplined for behavior that is characteristic of their disabling condition and are disproportionately disciplined relative to their peers (e.g., students receive demerits or office referrals for behaviors that are common for students with autism, such as demand avoidance or failure to follow first-time directions)
Respond to Inequity *Address the impact of the inequitable practice (e.g., educate, repair harm)*	♦ What steps can I take to change the policy so that it no longer disadvantages students with social, emotional, or behavioral disabilities?	♦ Create a policy that incorporates responses to behavior that are developmentally appropriate and not incompatible with student disabilities
Redress Inequity *Identify the root cause of the inequity and eliminate it*	♦ What organizational norms or traditions led to the inequitable policy? ♦ What underlying beliefs or mindsets led to the inequitable policies?	♦ Consequence-based rules are the norm, and teachers lack expertise in the science of behavior and supporting students with behavioral disabilities ♦ Examine existing school-wide and classroom discipline policies and teacher protocols with a collaborative team to identify how they might be harmful or not aligned with the needs of students with emotional or behavioral disabilities

(Continued)

TABLE 5.9 (CONTINUED) Equity Skills in a Person-First Culture

Equity Abilities	Reflection Question	Potential Response
Cultivate Equity *Develop and/or revise policies, protocols, practices, and procedures that promote justice for exceptional learners*	♦ What routines can be embedded into our daily schedule that incorporate strategies for effective behavior support? ♦ What common accommodations for students with emotional and behavioral disabilities should be integrated into our classroom and school-wide systems?	♦ Revise discipline policy and classroom protocols to incorporate developmentally appropriate, logical, and instructive responses to challenging behaviors with a focus on teaching prosocial behavior and improving social, emotional, and behavioral skills
Sustain Equity *Create support structures and accountability systems to maintain equity*	♦ What are the enabling conditions necessary to maintain social-emotional support systems that are empowering to exceptional learners and sustainable for teachers?	♦ Crosswalk all written policies and protocols to ensure alignment with the new policy ♦ Integrate step-back meetings to reflect on policy implementation into pre-existing data analysis protocols

Chapter Summary

Because of its focus on promoting belonging and well-being through proactive and positive systems, a *Person-First Culture* can transform school culture. Integrating supportive management systems, strategic relationship-building, social-emotional skill development, targeted interventions, and systems for well-being is integral to student academic and behavioral success. When utilized as part of a holistic approach to inclusivity, these five elements can create environments that promote success for students traditionally placed in self-contained classrooms or specialized schools.

The strategies outlined in this chapter will not work in isolation! They must be accompanied by an engaging and student-focused academic program, which we will explore in the next chapter.

> **REFLECT ON YOUR STUDENT**
>
> *Reflect*: Answer <u>one</u> of the following questions.
> 1. What core practices in this chapter can or could have transformed the experience of the student, Michael, at the beginning of this chapter?
> 2. Consider the student you identified at the beginning of this chapter. How could their experience be strengthened by the implementation of the practices in this chapter?

Your Role

The call to action for leaders is to:
Reframe disciple systems as social-emotional support systems

Each stakeholder has a crucial role in actively creating an anti-exclusionary and inclusive environment where every student can thrive. From principals who set the vision and hold stakeholders accountable to teachers who implement inclusive practices and parents who advocate for their child's needs, every individual has a part to play in this collective effort. Use Table 5.10 to identify the role you can play in answering the call to action for anti-exclusionary program design.

Tips for Parents

- **Ask about your school's approach to behavior.** Ask the school how it ensures educators know and understand how to effectively support student social-emotional well-being. Ask them what systems exist to build these skills for staff and students.
- **Learn about behavior.** Understand the different functions of behavior and the characteristics of a behavior-supportive home and school environment. Ask the school to provide learning opportunities on these topics.

TABLE 5.10 Stakeholder Roles: Person-First Culture

Stakeholder Role	*Reframe Discipline Systems as Social Emotional Support Systems*
School Leader (Principal, Executive Director, Assistant Principal, etc.)	♦ Ground discipline policies, procedures, and protocols in inclusive values and setting expectations aligned to those values. ♦ Build staff capacity to understand behavior science and effective behavior support. ♦ Create coaching systems to provide feedback to educators.
Principal Managers and District Leaders	♦ Set district-wide expectations around proactive and positive approaches to behavior. ♦ Allocate resources to support that vision.
Funders	♦ Develop funding priorities and requirements focused on are positive, proactive, and supportive behavior and discipline practices.
School Support Organizations	♦ Ensure that programming provided to schools regarding behavior, discipline, and mental health includes a focus on effectively supporting exceptional learners.
Policymakers	♦ Mandate practices, create policies, or offer incentives requiring schools to prioritize a proactive, positive, and supportive approach to behavior.
Families and Caregivers	♦ Educate yourself about proactive and positive behavior strategies. Collaborate with your child's school to develop strategies to strengthen your student's social, behavioral, or emotional skills.

From Knowing to Doing: Driving Change for a Person-First Culture

Transforming discipline and behavior systems is one of the most challenging leadership tasks. It is not enough to simply know the practices that define a Person-First Culture. Transformation requires systemic change. This is one key reason why true inclusivity continues to elude schools. Leaders must resist superficial changes and focus on analyzing mindsets, policies, and practices to determine how they prevent or promote belonging and well-being. Leaders can bridge the gap between knowing what to do and doing it through an action-oriented and strategic approach, as illustrated in previous chapters (Pfeffer & Sutton, 2000).

The considerations outlined in Table 5.11 can serve as a guide to help you effectively manage change and bridge the gap between knowing and doing.

TABLE 5.11 Change Management Considerations: Person-First Culture

Key Steps	Understand and Consider Your Context	Leader Actions
Lay the Foundation	*Identify Your Current State*	♦ Assess current discipline and classroom management systems to determine if they promote belonging and positive social-emotional outcomes. Use data to identify areas where traditional discipline methods might be hindering student success.
	Build Relationships and Trust	♦ Gather feedback from community members (teachers, caregivers, students, community members) and engage them in the evaluation process. Gather data from them related to the core practices of Person-First Culture.
	Engage Your Community	♦ Evaluate whether you have the necessary relationships to engage and empower members of your team, staff, and community to drive change in this area. ♦ Identify next steps for building key relationships and gaining the result of your community. Δ
Empower Key Stakeholders	*Build Capacity*	♦ Provide ongoing professional development focused on behavior science and effective social-emotional support practices. ♦ Create coaching systems to support implementation of proactive social-emotional support systems.
	Create a Compelling Vision	♦ Develop and communicate a vision that reframes discipline systems as social-emotional support systems. ♦ Ensure vision is grounded in common value and beliefs aligned to the school community's needs and aspirations.
	Create Systems of Support	♦ Address the emotional aspects of change. ♦ Be willing to make courageous decisions when there is misalignment.
	Be Driven by Action	♦ Be empathetic and intentional about addressing the concerns of those affected by the change. ♦ Provide necessary resources to support their ability to navigate the change.

(Continued)

TABLE 5.11 (CONTINUED) Change Management Considerations: Person-First Culture

Key Steps	Understand and Consider Your Context	Leader Actions
Focus on Outcomes	Use Data to Drive Decision-Making	♦ Set clear goals and create an action plan for each of the core practices aligned to your target area. Δ ♦ The framework in the appendix can be used as a self-reflection tool to guide goal setting.
	Align Policies and Practices	♦ Develop leading and lagging indicators to help monitor success and inform needed adjustments. Δ
Transform Systems	Ongoing Inquiry	♦ Align policies and practices to your vision and your commitment to equity. Relevant policies and practices may include hiring, staffing, scheduling, usage of resources, and design of the school environment. Δ ♦ Identify how existing policies and practices in this area may be perpetuating inequity for students with identified social, emotional, or behavioral needs. ♦ Transform systems so they align to the core practices of Person-First Culture, resist temporary or band-aid solutions. Δ
Continuous Improvement	Celebrate Success	♦ Create a system for ongoing inquiry to improve practices. Δ ♦ Elicit feedback from impacted stakeholders. ♦ Evaluate whether redesign or new policies and practices are creating or perpetuating inequity. ♦ Determine whether students with targeted social, emotional, or behavioral needs are making progress and benefiting from the new system. ♦ Be flexible and responsive to feedback. Δ
	Understand and Consider Your Context	♦ Share progress and successes with all stakeholders. ♦ Celebrate wins, milestones, and achievements to motivate staff and build momentum. Δ

Source: Tyack and Cuban (1995), Heath and Heath (2010), and Fullan (2016).

> **YOUR ROLE**
>
> *Reflect:* Answer both questions.
> 1. How has this chapter expanded your view on discipline and classroom management?
> 2. Which stakeholder role do you hold, and what will you do to commit to the call to action?

Action Planning

Now that you have a stronger understanding of inclusive discipline and management systems and social-emotional support systems, let us revisit your answer to our initial reflection question: "Are your systems inclusive?"

Table 5.12 is an expanded version of the table you saw at the beginning of this chapter. The nuance distinguishing typical action from disruptive status-quo-breaking action lies in the details. Review the shifts in the last column and answer the

TABLE 5.12 The Three Problems: Solutions for a Person-First Culture

Problem	Potential Solutions
The Ownership Problem *Are the correct individuals accountable for this challenge?*	◆ Shift responsibility to a collaborative team approach where all educators share ownership of student behavior support ◆ Train general educators to understand and address behavior need
The Design Problem *Does the design of the learning environment promote belonging and social-emotional well-being for exceptional learners?*	◆ Create classroom environments that support student self-regulation ◆ Teach students how to interact with peers and adults
The Knowledge Problem *Do all educators understand effective practice in this area?*	◆ Train general educators on the science of behavior ◆ Provide ongoing professional development focused on behavior support strategies ◆ Ensure coaching from leaders with expertise in behavior management

questions that follow. You will then use this reflection and your understanding of Person-First Culture to identify the next steps and begin action planning.

> **TRADITIONAL DISCIPLINE VS. PERSON-FIRST CULTURE**
>
> *Reflect*: How do these shifts vary from traditional systems design?

Planning Template

Planning Task	Notes
Final Reflection *How has this chapter expanded your view on equity? Revisit your answer to the first reflection question about the three sample learner profiles and respond with those profiles in mind.*	
Goal *Craft one goal aligned with the content of this chapter.*	
Resources *What resources are needed to meet this goal? Consider human capital, scheduling, and finances.*	

Bibliography

Campbell, J. (1999). *Student Discipline and Classroom Management*. Charles C Thomas Publisher, Ltd.

Carter, E. W., & Biggs, E. E. (2021). *Creating communities of belonging for students with significant cognitive disabilities (Belonging Series)*. Minneapolis, MN: University of Minnesota, TIES Center.

DuFour, R., DuFour, R., Eaker, R., Many, T., & Mattos, M. (2016). *Learning by doing: A handbook for professional learning communities at work* (3rd ed.). Solution Tree Press.

Emdin, C. (2016). *For White Folks Who Teach in the Hood... and the Rest of Y'all Too: Reality Pedagogy and Urban Education*. Beacon Press.

Fenning, P., & Jenkins, K. (2018). Racial and Ethnic Disparities in Exclusionary School Discipline: Implications for Administrators Leading Discipline Reform Efforts. *NASSP Bulletin*, 102(4), 291–302. DOI: 10.1177/0192636518812699

Fenning, Pamela, Theodos, Jennifer, Benner, Courtney, & Bohanon-Edmonson, Hank. (2004). Integrating proactive discipline practices into codes of conduct. *Journal of School Violence*, 3(1), 45–62.

Fullan, M. (2016). *Coherence: The right drivers in action for schools, districts, and systems*. Corwin Press.

Gorski, P., & Swalwell, K. (2023). Fix Injustice, Not Kids and Other Principles for Transformative Equity Leadership.

Greene, R. W. (2014a). *Lost at school: Why our kids with behavioral challenges are falling through the cracks and how we can help them* (Revised and updated ed.). Scribner.

Greene, R. W. (2014b). *The Explosive Child: A New Approach for Understanding and Parenting Easily Frustrated, Chronically Inflexible Children*. HarperCollins.

Greene, R., & Winkler, J. (2019). Collaborative & Proactive Solutions (CPS): A Review of Research Findings in Families, Schools, and Treatment Facilities. *Clinical Child and Family Psychology Review*, 22(4), 549–561. https://doi.org/10.1007/s10567-019-00295-z

Greene, R. W., Ablon, J. S., & Martin, A. (2006). Use of collaborative problem solving to reduce seclusion and restraint in child and adolescent inpatient units. *Psychiatric Services*, 57(5), 610–612. https://doi.org/10.1176/ps.2006.57.5.610

Heath, C., & Heath, D. (2010). *Switch: How to change things when change is hard*. Crown Business.

Hott, B. L., Jones, B. A., Rodriguez, J., Brigham, F. J., Martin, A., & Mirafuentes, M. (2021). Are Rural Students Receiving FAPE? A Descriptive Review of IEPs for Students with Social, Emotional, or Behavioral Needs. *Behavior Modification*, 45(1), 13–38. https://doi.org/10.1177/0145445518825107

Individuals with Disabilities Education Act, 20 U.S.C. § 1400 (2004).

Kelly, J., & Pohl, B. (2018). Using Structured Positive and Negative Reinforcement to Change Student Behavior in Educational Settings in order to Achieve Student Academic Success. *Multidisciplinary*

Journal for Education, Social and Technological Sciences, 5(1), 17–29. https://doi.org/10.4995/muse.2018.6370

Leverson, M., Smith, K., McIntosh, K., Rose, J., & Pinkelman, S. (2021). *PBIS cultural responsiveness field guide: Resources for trainers and coaches*. Center on PBIS, University of Oregon. https://www.pbis.org

Lewis, C. W., & Toldson, I. (Eds.). (2013). *Black male teachers : Diversifying the united states' teacher workforce*. Emerald Publishing Limited.

Liebtag, E. (2021). *Designing schools to support the whole child: A story of partnership*. Transcend, Inc and Van Ness Elementary School. Retrieved from https://transcendeducation.org/designing-schools-to-support-the-whole-child-a-story-of-partnership/

McIntosh, K., Girvan, E. J., McDaniel, S. C., Santiago-Rosario, M. R., St. Joseph, S., Falcon, S. F., Izzard, S., & Bastable, E. (2021). Effects of an equity-focused PBIS approach to school improvement on exclusionary discipline and school climate. *Preventing School Failure: Alternative Education for Children and Youth*, 65(4), 354–361. DOI: 10.1080/1045988X.2021.1937027

Minahan, J., & Rappaport, N. (2012). *The behavior code: A practical guide to understanding and teaching the most challenging students*. Harvard Education Press.

Pfeffer, J., & Sutton, R. I. (2000). The knowing-doing problem. *Harvard Business Review*, 78(2), 108–119.

RAND Corporation. (2024). Teacher well-being and intentions to leave in 2024: Findings from the 2024 State of the American Teacher survey. RAND Corporation. https://www.rand.org/pubs/research_reports/RRA1108-12.html

Simonsen, B. & George, H.P. (2022). Supporting inclusive practices with positive behavioral interventions and supports. In J. McLeskey, N. L. Waldron, F. Spooner, & B. Algozzine (Eds.), *Handbook of effective inclusive elementary schools* (2nd ed., pp. 139–163). Routledge.

Transforming School Discipline Collaborative. (n.d.). *TSDC toolkit: Model school code*. https://www.transformschooldiscipline.org/tsdc-toolkit#anchor-model-code

Tyack, D., & Cuban, L. (1995). *Tinkering toward utopia: A century of public school reform*. Harvard University Press.

United States Government Accountability Office. (2018). K-12 education: Discipline disparities for Black students, boys, and students with disabilities (GAO-18-258). https://www.gao.gov/products/gao-18-258

U.S. Department of Education, Institute of Education Sciences, National Center for Education Statistics. (2024). Back to School Responses to COVID-19. https://ies.ed.gov/schoolsurvey/spp/

U.S. Department of Education. (2022). Positive, proactive approaches to supporting children with disabilities: A guide for stakeholders. https://sites.ed.gov/idea/files/guide-positive-proactive-approaches-to-supporting-children-with-disabilities.pdf

U.S. News & World Report. (2024). Best education administration programs. https://www.usnews.com/best-graduate-schools/top-education-schools/education-administration-rankings

Whole Child Model. (n.d.). Homepage. https://www.wholechildmodel.org

Wriston, B., & Duchesneau, N. (2023). *How school discipline impacts students' social, emotional, and academic development (SEAD)*. The Education Trust.

6

Principle 4

Student-Centered Instruction

The call to action for leaders is to:
Disrupt general education so all kids can learn.

Old Thinking: Students with learning needs are best supported by special educators.
New Thinking: The general education classroom should support learner variability.

In This Section

At first glance, the quote, "If we fixed general education, we would not need special education," may seem controversial, even off-putting for many special education advocates. But hear me out. Special education came about because students with disabilities were being discriminated against and not supported at school. General education was not doing enough. What if instead of this resulting in the passing of a law to guarantee support for certain students, leaders approached the challenges with the attitude, "What does this student need? Let's figure out how to meet that need."

What if, instead of isolating supports in separate programs, schools integrated them into their overall approach, making them a fundamental part of how they do business?

Do certain students need targeted and specialized support? Absolutely. But, as I have said throughout this book, "special education" in its current form isn't "special" because it's not doing what it needs to do. This is why I argue we need an evolved approach toward systems design, especially our instructional systems. This starts with normalizing the idea that every learner is different and can achieve regardless of that difference.

Instruction is the number one factor in student achievement, and our instructional systems are not designed to support diverse learners—gifted learners, culturally diverse learners, multilingual learners, and especially not students with disabilities. If we don't shift our approach to instruction and operate with an increased level of intensity and urgency, we will perpetuate inequity for exceptional learners.

The core practices of *Student-Centered Instruction* are as follows:

- Tiered Instruction
- Universally Designed Grade-Level Instruction
- Personalized Learning Structures
- Targeted Interventions
- High-Quality Specialized Instruction

After reading this chapter, you might think, "These are not innovative new practices. How is this different from what I've already heard?" The reality is that they may be known, but they are seldom implemented (Levenson, 2011). As you navigate this chapter, consider each practice with an evaluative lens. To what degree is this practice evident in my context, why do gaps exist, and how do I need to intensify my work in this area?

> **CHAPTER CONTENTS**
>
> - The Three Problems in Instruction
> - Student Story: Chas
> - The General Education Classroom Needs to Evolve
> - Learner Variability and Instruction
> - Core Practices
> - From Knowing to Doing: Driving Change for Student-Centered Instruction
> - Action Planning
> - Coaches Toolkit

Reflecting on the *Three Problems* in Instructional Systems

Are your classrooms truly academically inclusive? Are they promoting strong academic outcomes for your exceptional learners? If not, why? In Chapter 1, we explored three problems that may represent the answer to that question: the *Ownership Problem*, the *Design Problem*, and the *Knowledge Problem*. Let's start our exploration of instructional systems by considering them through the lens of these problems. Review Table 6.1 and consider how they manifest in your school's systems.

Did your reflection reveal that these problems are evident within your systems? If so, it is likely due to the reality that what we are doing is not working. Several realities have sounded the alarm for change:

- Leading scholars have warned that "schools fail to provide sufficiently intensive instruction" (Fuchs et al., 2018).
- In 2017, the Supreme Court addressed the need for schools to take greater responsibility in driving meaningful academic growth for students with disabilities (Endrew F., 2017).

TABLE 6.1 The Three Problems: Instruction

Problem	Common Examples in Instructional Systems
The Ownership Problem *Are the right individuals accountable for this challenge?*	◆ Nonexperts in literacy/math expected to close gaps for students with disabilities ◆ Interventions provided by those without content expertise ◆ Special educators lack coaching from literacy/math experts
The Design Problem *Does the design of the learning environment promote belonging and social-emotional well-being for exceptional learners?*	◆ Segregated schools, programs, and classrooms are primarily the result of adult beliefs and actions, not student needs ◆ Many special education students receive support in resource rooms ◆ Special education students are pulled aside by special educators for math and reading supports ◆ Schedule does not allow for receipt of grade-level instruction by content expert AND the amount of remedial instruction necessary to promote growth
The Knowledge Problem *Do all educators understand effective practice in this area?*	◆ Students with specific math and reading disabilities receive specialized instruction from educators lacking content expertise ◆ Limited professional development focused on evidence-based practices for teaching students with disabilities ◆ General educators do not understand the neurodevelopmental framework and how to design lessons that support learner variability ◆ Special educators may lack content-specific strategies for teaching literacy and math

◆ A 2023 research study showed that the impact of special education services on academic achievement is nonsignificant, specifically noting, "special education services alone may not be sufficiently intensive to improve academic achievement" (Woods et al., 2023).

To address these challenges, we must reexamine our approach to instruction through the lens of collective accountability, a value introduced earlier in this book. This belief represents the idea that "every kid is my kid" and emphasizes that responsibility for exceptional learners should not be limited to specialist teachers and leaders. This next section challenges you to consider how embracing this value is essential to transforming general education classrooms, a critical step in fulfilling our duty to exceptional learners.

Student Story: Chas

Kate McElligott shared with me the inspiring story of Chas, a testament to the power of the belief that "every kid is my kid." In her senior English IV class, students were diving into *Heart of Darkness*, exploring the deep themes of imperialism and colonialism, while Chas, a student with a significant disability, fully participated in the discussions. Though Chas's disability sometimes meant his communication was brief and unclear, his contributions always resonated with his peers, often bringing laughter to the group.

Chas's positive academic journey was possible because of the careful collaboration between his special education and general education teachers, who committed to ensuring he had access to the same rigorous content as his classmates. His learning materials were thoughtfully adapted—whether through simplified vocabulary or alternative ways to respond—empowering him to engage meaningfully with the same topics and skills necessary for college readiness.

This inclusive approach didn't just support Chas; it also enriched the classroom for everyone involved. Other students who previously struggled with maintaining focus, became more engaged when they took on the role of supporting Chas. Their involvement not only helped Chas thrive but also boosted their performance in class.

Chas's story highlights the importance of providing students with disabilities access to the general education classroom and rigorous content. His inclusion was about more than fairness; it was about equipping him with the skills needed to achieve his most ambitious post-high school goals in supported employment and living. Let Chas's story be a guide as we dive into this chapter on instruction, where I will ask you to lean into the mindset, "Every kid is my kid," as we examine how to design learning environments where all students, regardless of their abilities, can contribute, learn, and succeed together.

The General Education Classroom Needs to Evolve

Who deserves the best teachers? Who deserves to be in the "regular" classroom? Who is smart enough for grade-level or advanced content? Leaders make decisions about who deserves what every day through their design of instructional systems. Practices, policies, and protocols such as the schedule, assignment of teachers, curriculum, and instructional expectations are among the greatest barriers to the success of exceptional learners.

Schools often claim to be inclusive yet maintain instructional practices that do not meet the needs of exceptional learners. These include whole-group instruction, rigid pacing, and text-heavy worksheets, to name a few. School leaders and general education teachers control the design of the instructional setting, where 70% of students with disabilities spend 80% of their time. Even though most of their time is spent in general education, accountability for meeting their needs rests primarily on the shoulders of special education teachers and leaders, who have limited authority and limited capacity.

The responsibility must shift to include school leaders and general education teachers. Those who design instructional systems have the power to either perpetuate or prevent the failure of exceptional learners. If leaders shift their perspective from focusing on leading school to leading learning, they can interrupt this failure. Some questions leaders can ask themselves to support this shift are as follows:

- ◆ Do I advocate for deep learning for all students?
- ◆ Does our approach to instruction for all learners reflect an understanding of the concept of learning?
- ◆ Do our systems provide the emotional conditions for learning for exceptional learners?

This shift must be accompanied by an evolved general education model that is designed to support learner variability. This evolution should include the use of evidence-based and universally designed curricula, accessible grade-level content, structures that allow content experts to remediate essential skill gaps, specially designed high-quality instruction for exceptional learners, systems that allow teachers to assess progress frequently, and monitoring of the effectiveness of these practices.

Is Efficiency More Important than Outcomes?

The practices named earlier are high-leverage practices, evidence-based, and proven to drive outcomes for diverse learner types, yet elusive to a critical mass of schools. Why is this the case? Might it be the prioritization of efficiency over outcomes for *all* learner types? Many factors drive this focus on efficiency—finite resources, economies of scale, or systemic design flaws. However, the implications are profound, exclusionary practices that segregate subgroups of students, depriving them of the structures essential to academic growth—grade-level instruction, grade-level peer models, and content experts.

Consider the examples in Figure 6.1. Which examples exist in your context, typical or transformative?

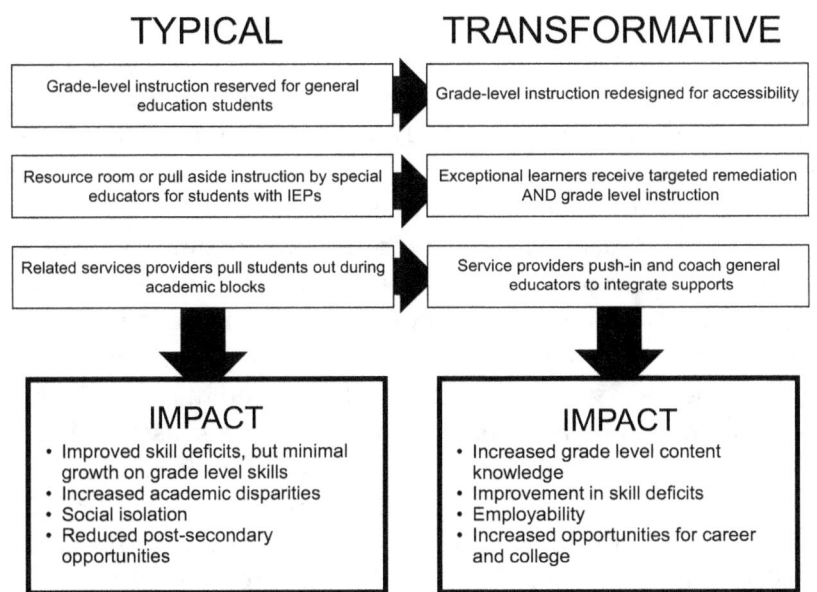

FIGURE 6.1 Efficiency vs. Outcomes - Comparison of typical vs. transformative approaches to inclusive education.

Do you want to be efficient, or do you want to serve kids? I agree with those who push that it is disingenuous to pretend that simply providing accommodations or integrating evidence-based practice into a general education lesson alone is sufficient for students who are years behind their peers (Sayeski et al., 2019). An evolved approach requires "integration in the regular classroom **and** an individualized special education *calculated to achieve advancement from grade to grade.*" The emphasis on "and" is intentional here. Remember, I said the nuance is in the details. First, students need both general education instruction *in addition to* special education supports. Second, special education supports "calculated to achieve advancement" articulates an increased standard that asks educators to ensure those supports are designed to deliberately promote grade-level academic achievement. The practices outlined in this chapter, taken together, can help leaders meet this heightened expectation. Let's dive in by looking at a school committed to service over efficiency, working to transform and disrupt traditional systems.

The Danger of Low Expectations

"Why can't I go to college like Darryl?" This is a question I am frequently asked by my nephew, Isaiah, who just completed 12th grade at Accel Academy, a private school for students with significant disabilities. He is a 17-year-old student with autism who watches honors chemistry videos on YouTube and constantly asks why he can't attend college like his cousin Darryl. At his last IEP meeting, his advocate asked about his academic programming, knowing that Isaiah wanted to study biology and advanced math topics. The response was, "he has a low IQ score, and he's not going to be able to attend college. If you want him to learn academics, you must take him to a different school." There are so many problems with that response, a discussion that I'll reserve for my next book, but the reality is that he was at a different school, a school that said, "We can't serve his IEP in the regular classroom, and we don't have a classroom that matches his IEP so we will put his desk in the hallway."

Isaiah's plight is representative of many students with needs who educators don't know how to or are unwilling to support.

Isaiah is a bright and motivated teenager who, if you ask him, "How old will I be in the year 2063," can answer you in a millisecond as you sit there and try to compute the math yourself. By the time you think to yourself, "I'm 47, the year is..." he has already answered "97." Imagine if Isaiah's school recognized this brilliance and leveraged it as an opportunity instead of focusing on his challenges.

As the learning leader in your school, you *must* establish and hold teachers accountable for setting high academic expectations for students like Isaiah. To do otherwise is to actively fail these learners. There is little argument that low expectations have a detrimental impact on the growth of all learners, but especially students with disabilities.

In *Hidden Potential*, Adam Grant highlights the detrimental impact of low expectations, "the expectations people hold of us often become self-fulfilling prophecies," and in schools, when teachers hold high expectations for students, they "get smarter and earn higher grades—especially if they start out with disadvantages" (2023). Isaiah is precisely the student Grant was talking about. Learning science underscores the need for high expectations; the Professional Standards for Educational Leaders (PSEL) mandate them, and the research referenced throughout this book echoes it.

The least dangerous assumption states that if we aren't 100% sure of a student's potential or abilities, we should make decisions that, if wrong, have the fewest negative repercussions against the person. Instead of a deficit mindset, educators should view kids like Isaiah through a lens of capability and create an environment designed to support rigorous goal attainment.

Here are some misconceptions I've heard about neurodivergent students and students with disabilities (Figure 6.2).

Which have you heard? Which do you believe? One of the most heard sentiments is, "Those kids can't learn grade-level instruction!" A belief that has led to separate classes, programs, and schools not just for neurodivergent students and those with disabilities but also for gifted students, multilingual learners, and others who don't fit the mold of the "average" learner. The truth is, rigorous instruction is essential to the academic

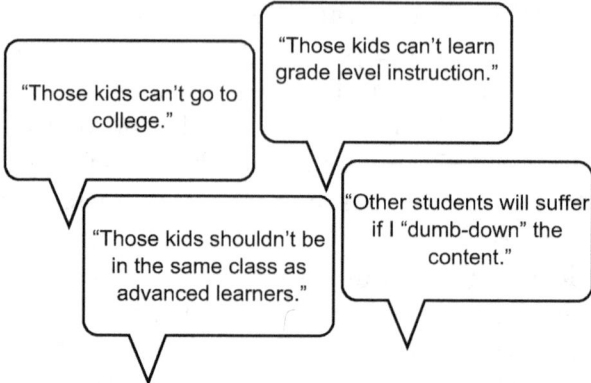

FIGURE 6.2 Challenging Deficit-Based Beliefs About Students with Disabilities. This figure highlights common deficit-based assumptions about students with disabilities, emphasizing the need to confront and replace these harmful narratives with a belief in every student's potential to succeed.

growth of every one of these student groups, but especially for the nontraditional learner (Hammond, 2015; U.S. Department of Education, 2015; Grant, 2023).

From Exclusion to Universal Participation

Let me be frank: specialized classrooms, programs, and schools are exclusionary. They do not promote rigorous post-secondary outcomes for students with disabilities, and they perpetuate segregation in our society. "[S]chooling has traditionally been configured to shape the macrocosm society, and its focus on differentiating between able-bodied and disabled people. The result has been a historically inflexible system, largely intolerant of children who do not—or cannot—'fit' into school cultures, who then become relegated to specially designated classrooms, schools and institutions" (Connor, 2014). Students with disabilities are more successful in inclusive classrooms than in segregated settings and are five times more likely to graduate than those who are not.

Along with other inclusive education advocates, I am advocating for systemic change in special education. Its current iteration has run its course. Did you know that there are policies, legislation, and judicial mandates that require the inclusion of students with disabilities? The law governing special education specifically states that education agencies must ensure that "[a] child with a disability is not removed from education in age-appropriate regular classrooms solely because of needed modifications in the general education curriculum" (U.S. Department of Education, n.d.). This means we should not be placing students in resource rooms or self-contained classrooms because the student needs academic modifications. This is contrary to what is happening in many schools. Many students, particularly those with intellectual disabilities, continue to receive their services in segregated educational settings (Taylor et al., 2020).

Exceptional learners deserve to be in the classroom with their general education peers and can be successful in the regular classroom, but no matter how many times this is said, effective inclusive classrooms continue to elude educators (Billingsley et al., 2022). So, how do we go from exclusion to universal participation? Exclusion represents the idea that certain students are removed from the general education classroom because there is a mismatch between the classroom environment and their needs. Universal participation ensures that all students participate in the general education setting because it is designed to support the needs of the "universe" of students or all students.

Making the shift from exclusion to universal participation is possible through the strategic alignment of instructional systems to this goal. These factors are addressed in this and the other chapters in this book.

- **High Expectations for Exceptional Learners**: Maintain and communicate high expectations for all students, including those with intellectual disabilities.
- **Rigorous Goals**: Establish and maintain rigorous academic goals for exceptional learners to ensure they are challenged and supported to achieve their full potential.
- **Accessible Grade-Level Instruction**: Guarantee that all students, including those with disabilities, have access to grade-level instruction. Select and adapt a curriculum that is inclusive and accessible, incorporating diverse perspectives and being flexible to meet the needs of students with various abilities and backgrounds.

- **Tiered Supports:** Provide tiered support to address student needs, ensuring that each learner receives the appropriate level of intervention and assistance.
- **Flexible Instructional Blocks:** Avoid traditional instructional blocks that prioritize whole-group instruction and standardized pacing. Instead, design instructional blocks that are flexible and responsive to the needs of all learners.
- **Educator Capacity Building:** Focus on building educator capacity around learner variability through professional development and ongoing support.
- **Accountability and Feedback:** Continuously support the implementation of inclusive practices through regular observation and constructive feedback.

Application: Shawn, Darryl, and Isaiah

> *Reflect*: *Let's consider these ingredients in the context of our learner profiles (Figure 2.1). Which of these ingredients, if missing, would likely result in Isaiah or Shawn being excluded from general education? What would it take to prevent this from happening in your own context?*

Learner Profiles

Shawn
- Resilient and motivated learner
- Has dyslexia (struggles with spelling and reading fluency)
- Experiences low mood, anger, and defensiveness
- Thrives in a positive and supportive environment

Isaiah
- Strong long-term memory and motivated to learn
- Requires structure, routines, and positive reinforcement
- Has Autism (uneven cognitive skills, stimming, and repetitive behaviors)
- Lagging skills in emotional regulation (managing frustration)

Darryl
- Highly motivated, independent worker who grasps complex concepts well
- Proficient in reading, math, and science
- Has ADD (fidgets and seeks touch stimulation)
- Resilient and collaborative learner

FIGURE 2.1 Learner Profiles for Tailored Instruction. This figure presents profiles of three diverse learners—Shawn, Isaiah, and Darryl—highlighting their strengths, challenges, and specific needs.

Learner Variability and Instruction

In Chapter 1, I introduced a neurodevelopmental framework for understanding learning and highlighted how the common demands of schooling can mismatch with student strengths and needs across domains like attention, memory, higher-order thinking (HOT), language, and social cognition. Let's revisit these domains as we prepare to consider the core practices of instructional systems that accommodate variability in these areas.

> **LEARNER VARIABILITY AND YOUR INSTRUCTIONAL SYSTEMS**
>
> *Reflect*: Review Table 6.2 and answer <u>one</u> of the following questions.
> 1. How do your curriculum and lesson planning address student needs in the various neurodevelopmental domains?
> 2. Are your teachers equipped to design lessons that support students facing challenges in these areas?

The core practices outlined next define the characteristics of an instructional system that is attentive to and designed around variability in the domains noted in this table. It is essential for educators to know and understand these domains and the following core practices as they seek to design instructional systems with this variability in mind.

Understanding Learner Variability in Literacy

Meeting the academic needs of exceptional learners requires educators to understand the various ways students may struggle with reading. Students with reading challenges typically struggle with reading accuracy, fluency, or comprehension. While many people are familiar with dyslexia, its characteristics are not commonly understood or properly supported in schools. Individuals with dyslexia may struggle with recognizing sounds, decoding words, reading fluently, spelling, writing, or comprehension (Understood, n.d.-b). Additionally, educators should be aware

TABLE 6.2 Neurodevelopmental Domains of Learning

Domain	Indicators of Strength (If This System Is Strong, Students Can)	Common Demands of School
Attention	♦ Maintain and regulate cognitive energy and alertness over a learning period ♦ Process and sort incoming information ♦ Planning, organizing, and producing output at an appropriate pace	♦ Listening to lectures ♦ Completing independent work ♦ Turning in assignments on time
HOT	♦ Make connections across content areas ♦ Interpret and make sense of new ideas ♦ Make inferences ♦ Engage in creative thinking ♦ Engage in systematic problem-solving	♦ Completing projects or experiments ♦ Completing assignments ♦ Analyzing texts and problems
Language	♦ Process and understand oral and written information (receptive language) ♦ Communicate and produce ideas orally and in writing (expressive language)	♦ Following instructions ♦ Completing written assignments
Memory	♦ Store and retrieve information (long-term memory) ♦ Mentally juggle information while using it (working memory)	♦ Remember historical facts ♦ Remember math facts, procedures, and rules
Social Cognition	♦ Navigate interactions with peers ♦ Respond appropriately during social settings ♦ Interpret others' emotions ♦ Collaborate with peers	♦ Working in small groups ♦ Participating in class discussions ♦ Interacting during extracurriculars ♦ Group projects

Source: Barringer et al. (2010).

of other reading disabilities, such as hyperlexia and dysgraphia (see Table 6.3). Students with reading challenges may also experience related issues, like expressive language disorders (difficulty communicating thoughts) or receptive language disorders (difficulty understanding spoken words).

TABLE 6.3 Learner Variability in Literacy

Disorder	Characteristics
Dyslexia	◆ *Primary Challenges*: decoding, fluency, and spelling ◆ *Potential Impacts*: comprehension, writing
Hyperlexia	◆ *Primary Challenges*: comprehension, advanced word recognition, and/or fluency
Dysgraphia	◆ *Primary Challenges*: word production and handwriting ◆ *Potential Impact*: spelling, expressive language

Source: American Speech-Language-Hearing Association (n.d.) and International Dyslexia Association (n.d.).

Oftentimes, reading challenges are coupled with difficulties related to processing or memory. Processing needs can impact reading fluency and the amount of time it takes students to consume information and process it. Depending upon the context, this can result in poor academic performance. Students with ADHD, for example, may have weak working memory, which means they struggle with consuming information and holding on to it. In a reading classroom, this can present challenges when it comes to reading and comprehending large amounts of text. What is critical is that educators understand the student's specific area of challenge and appropriate strategies for supporting students in that area and remediating skill deficits.

Many common accommodations for students with reading challenges can be integrated class-wide to better support a range of reading needs and can benefit all students (see Table 6.4). Systematically integrating these accommodations into lesson and classroom design can mitigate known challenges for many students and make the integration of targeted supports more manageable for teachers.

Understanding Learner Variability in Math

Math learning needs vary greatly from student to student. Students with math disabilities are typically classified as having a Specific Learning Disability in Math. Dyscalculia is the broad category typically used to describe individuals with math challenges. Students may have only one or several of the characteristics of dyscalculia. Educators should understand each student's individual challenges to identify appropriate supports.

TABLE 6.4 Common Accommodations

Materials and Routines	Instructions
◆ Use strips or bookmarks to help focus when reading ◆ Large-print text in handouts ◆ Use audiobooks ◆ Text readers ◆ Speech-to-text software ◆ Extended time for reading and writing ◆ Opportunities to re-read ◆ Partner reading structures	◆ Written and spoken instructions ◆ Simplified directions ◆ Highlight keywords and ideas in handouts ◆ Provide exemplars ◆ Provide rubrics ◆ Chunked assignments ◆ Self-monitoring checklists ◆ Scaffolded questions from easiest to hardest
Introducing New Concepts	**Assignments**
◆ Pre-teach new concepts and vocabulary ◆ Written notes or outlines ◆ Advance organizers to help students organize ideas during lessons ◆ Glossaries	◆ Sentence starters ◆ Options for demonstrating understanding ◆ Focus grading on priority skills

Source: Understood (n.d.-a).

Common characteristics of dyscalculia include the following (Understood, n.d.-a):

- *Primary Challenges*: number sense, quantity differentiation, calculating, estimating, use of math symbols
- *Potential Impacts*: problem-solving, reading graphical representations
- *Support Strategies*: number lines, manipulatives, visualization tools, additional time, explicit strategy instruction

Student-Centered Instruction: Core Practices

As you navigate this next section, be reminded, the nuance is in the details. Many schools are already implementing one or more of the core practices outlined in Table 6.5, but an instructional program that improves outcomes for exceptional learners requires higher levels of intensity and is a sum of *all* parts.

There are five core practices of *Student-Centered Instruction*:

TABLE 6.5 Core Practices: Student-Centered Instruction

Core Practice	Description
Tiered Instruction	A continuum of instruction rooted in high-quality core instruction for all students targeted small-group interventions for those needing additional help, and intensive individualized interventions for those not responding to the core and targeted instruction.
Universally Designed Grade-Level Instruction	Proactively designing instruction to be accessible for students across a range of abilities by anticipating barriers and designing for learner variability.
Personalized Learning Structures	Flexible academic structures that cater to the individual needs of students through differentiated instruction, flexible pacing, and alternative pathways or various routes for students to engage in learning based on their readiness, learning profiles, and needs.
Targeted Interventions	Intensive (higher frequency and duration) individualized skill remediation that supplements, rather than replaces, grade-level instruction, using evidence-based strategies such as one-on-one tutoring and small-group instruction.
High-Quality Specialized Instruction	Effective, evidence-based instructional strategies tailored to meet the unique needs of students with disabilities. Targeted supports should ensure instruction is both effective and aligned with IDEA mandates.

Core Practice 1: Tiered Instruction

Description: A continuum of instruction rooted in high-quality core instruction for all students, targeted small-group interventions for those needing additional help, and intensive individualized interventions for those not responding to the core and targeted instruction.

At the foundation of a student-centered approach to instruction is providing a continuum of supports that integrates prevention, intervention, monitoring, evaluation, and continuous improvement. Instruction and assessment across this continuum should be tiered as determined by an assessment of student needs. A tiered approach to instruction benefits all students and is especially critical to the success of exceptional learners. As we seek to normalize the notion that all learners vary and schools should be designed around that variability, we must normalize tiered instruction. For our purposes, tiered instruction, as defined by the IRIS Center (a leading technical assistance resource for educators) is

- high-quality standards-based core instruction provided to all students (Tier 1),
- supplemental small-group intervention for students unsuccessful in Tier 1 (Tier 2), and then
- intensive (e.g. increased number of sessions/session duration) interventions for nonresponsive students (Tier 3; IRIS Center, n.d.).

The concept of tiered instruction is anchored in the framework of MTSS, Multi-Tiered Systems of Support. This section is not about MTSS. As stated in an earlier chapter, I don't want you to get stuck on the notion of "another framework" or "another initiative." The goal of this section is to describe the characteristics of effective instruction that improve outcomes for exceptional learners, and one of those is *tiered instruction*. It is necessary, however, to name MTSS as the premise for these practices.

Tiered Intervention Example (Isaiah)
- Tier 1 – All kids receive 90 minutes of reading instruction
- Tier 2 – During the 90-minute reading block, instead of silent reading time, Isaiah spends 30 minutes twice a week using Lexia, an online reading program, or in a small group
- Tier 3 – In addition to the 90-minute reading block, Isaiah receives three weekly 45-minute 1:1 sessions with a reading interventionist using an evidence-based curriculum

High-Leverage Practices for Inclusive Classrooms
There are 22 high-leverage practices (HLP) for inclusive classrooms that every leader should know, set expectations around, and monitor to create truly inclusive classrooms (McLeskey et al., 2022a; see Figure 6.3). Most principals are not familiar with them, and they are not consistently present in classrooms. These practices have been intentionally integrated throughout the core practices outlined in this book and are not referenced as

HIGH-LEVERAGE PRACTICES FOR STUDENTS WITH DISABILITIES

Collaborate		Use Data to Plan	Instruct on Behavior and Academics	Intervene and Intensify
HLP 1 Collaborate with professionals	HLP 3 Collaborate with families	HLP 6 Use assessment information, analyze instruction, adjust as needed	HLP 7 Create consistent, organized, and responsive learning environments	HLP 20 Provide intensive intervention for academics and behavior
			HLP 16 Use explicit instruction	

Pillars

Embedded Practices

HLP 2: Organize and facilitate effective meetings with professionals and families

HLP 4: Use multiple information sources to develop a comprehensive picture of student strengths and student needs.
HLP 5: Interpret and share data. Use data to collaborative design academic and behavior programs.
HLP 11: Identify and prioritize learning goals (long-term and short-term)
HLP 12: Systematically design instruction aligned to learning goals.

What to Teach
HLP 9: Teach social behaviors
HLP 14: Teach cognitive and metacognitive strategies
HLP 21: Teach how to maintain and generalize new learning across time and settings
How to Teach
HLP 13: Adapt tasks and materials
HLP 15: Scaffolded academic and behavior supports
HLP 17: Flexible grouping
HLP 18: Promote active engagement
HLP 19: Assistive & Instructional technology
HLP 8/22: Positive and constructive feedback

HLP 10: Conduct functional behavioral assessments to inform individualized behavior plans

FIGURE 6.3 High-Leverage Practices for Students with Disabilities. This figure illustrates key pillars and embedded practices essential for supporting students with disabilities, emphasizing research-backed strategies that drive meaningful academic and social outcomes.

a separate list of expectations. The goal is to help leaders view instructional systems holistically and not as a set of disconnected practices across multiple frameworks. The remainder of this section will outline the core practices that define Student-Centered Instruction, which are grounded in the MTSS framework.

Core Practice 2: Universally Designed Grade-Level Instruction

Description: Proactively design instruction to be accessible for students across a range of abilities by anticipating barriers and designing for learner variability.

Effective tiered instruction starts with high-quality general education instruction (Courtade et al., 2022; Novak, 2022). High-quality general education instruction is defined as engaging and relevant content, differentiated instruction, ongoing formative assessment, culturally responsive teaching, evidence-based practices, and strong classroom management (Marzano, 2003; Danielson, 2007; Darling-Hammond, 2010; Hammond, 2015; McLeskey et al., 2022b). These elements make learning accessible for learners across the spectrum of ability by being universally designed to remove barriers to learning. If schools prioritize improving the core general education curriculum, they can significantly reduce the number of students who need more intensive intervention.

By now, you are likely familiar with the origin of accessibility ramps, present on sidewalks, walkways, and other entryways, designed to support individuals who need easier access due to mobility challenges. Not only did that accommodation support those individuals, but while not designed for them, it also supports access for strollers and other wheeled objects. This is an example of a design that increases access for a wider range of individuals. This concept should be applied to instruction in schools through the framework known as Universal Design for Learning (UDL). UDL helps educators make learning accessible for various learner types by asking them to proactively design lessons that anticipate variability by identifying barriers to learning and integrating strategies that promote increased understanding and engagement. *UDL must no longer be considered optional.*

I'm not going to go into the nitty gritty details of UDL because my experience coaching leaders in this area has revealed the complexity and challenge of making sense of it in conjunction with other pedagogy and frameworks leaders are expected to know (e.g., Danielson, Teach Like a Champion, etc.). The focus is on the practices themselves, as opposed to the title of the framework and its technical terminology.

There are three guidelines that educators can apply to maximize instructional accessibility for the range of learners in a classroom or universally design instruction.

- *Engage Learners* by welcoming their interests and identities, helping them sustain effort and motivation, and considering options for emotional growth.
- *Strengthen Understanding* by presenting and providing information in multiple ways.
- *Empower Students to Demonstrate Learning* by providing options for action and expression (Novak, 2016; CAST, 2024).

Engage Learners

Learners vary in the ways they can engage in learning and what motivates them to learn, and there are three common challenges that impact a teacher's ability to engage learners:

- Learners vary in what attracts their attention and maintains their interest.
- Learners vary in their ability to regulate their attention to complete tasks or maintain consistent effort over an instructional period.
- Learners vary in their ability to modulate emotional reactions and mental states to cope and engage with learning environments.

To address these challenges, educators must design lessons that integrate interests, include strategies to sustain motivation, and leverage strategies that support emotional well-being during lessons. The *UDL Toolkit* outlines strategies to support the aforementioned challenges and promote increased engagement (see online appendix at QR code in "Introduction"). This toolkit can be used by leaders to inform the design of lesson planning protocols, used in teacher coaching meetings, or leveraged during teacher observations.

Strengthen Understanding

Learners vary in how they perceive and make meaning of information presented to them. To support understanding of various learner types, teachers should present information in multiple ways and offer various options for interacting with learning materials. Doing so attends to varying learning styles, preferences, and abilities. Educators can leverage this as an opportunity to honor the diverse backgrounds and cultures of their students, a critical element of an equitable instructional approach (Fritzgerald, 2020). The three common challenges that impact a teacher's ability to strengthen understanding are as follows:

- Information presented in one modality (e.g., focuses on hearing, sight, or touch) presents barriers to access and comprehension
- Learners struggle to comprehend linguistic or nonlinguistic representations (e.g., vocabulary, symbols, expressions)
- Learners struggle to construct meaning and generate new understandings

Understanding is demonstrated through objective mastery and goal attainment. To strengthen understanding, teachers must provide alternative ways for students to process information using multiple modalities, varied cognitive and metacognitive strategies to support information processing, and strategically designed graduated scaffolds.

Scaffolding is key to supporting student processing and knowledge acquisition. Educators must understand that scaffolds must be designed to allow access without removing rigor. When leaders are observing classrooms and giving teachers feedback, this is a key look-for. Leaders should be prepared to coach teachers on how to adjust and remove scaffolds to encourage independence. Special educators can be especially susceptible to overusing scaffolds. Hammond (2015) refers to this as being a "sentimentalists," the goal is to help, but in reality, teachers end up hindering progress. To support teachers in this area, leaders should integrate reflections and planning for scaffolds into coaching meetings or planning protocols.

Empower Students to Demonstrate Learning

Learners vary in how they best demonstrate what they know. Many times, students understand a concept, but the way we assess student understanding creates a barrier to them demonstrating that knowledge. The three common challenges that impact a student's ability to demonstrate their learning are as follows:

- Students with specific challenges (e.g., dysgraphia, blindness, deafness) struggle with navigating provided tools, technology, or information presented in certain formats.
- Students are unable to express understanding using a particular modality (e.g., written, verbal).
- Students are unable to complete tasks or do not understand the necessary steps to complete tasks.

To best understand whether students have mastered a concept, educators must give students options for action and expression. Providing students with multiple ways to demonstrate their knowledge and skills honors their individuality, a key ingredient of an equity-centered approach (Fritzgerald, 2020). Options may include varying methods for response, use of assistive technology, varied tools and manipulatives (e.g., text-to-speech, calculators, virtual manipulatives), and scaffolds to support executive functions.

Making instruction accessible through universal design is a powerful strategy for supporting the various learner types that exist in a classroom and particularly essential to

> Is your current approach to grade-level instruction sufficiently intensive to promote growth for exceptional learners?

improving outcomes for students with significant intellectual and developmental disabilities. Typically, special education teachers are asked to be on double duty: first, analyze grade-level content to make it digestible, and then further break it down to target individual needs. By making instruction accessible from the onset, differentiation by special educators becomes more manageable and targeted. Universal design must become the standard approach to instruction, as educators seek to create engaging classrooms where every kind of learner thrives.

Intensity Pulse Check
- *Is your current approach to <u>instructional design</u> sufficiently intensive to promote growth for exceptional learners? What gaps exist between your approach and the core practices outlined in this section?*

Make Accommodations Classroom-Wide
Another transformative approach to increasing instructional accessibility is to embed accommodations, typically reserved for students with disabilities, into general instructional expectations. As a matter of fact, many typically used accommodations are strategies that, if used, align with strategies to support universally designed instruction. Would you rather receive written instructions or instructions spoken aloud? Would you rather take notes or use a recording device to record the lecture? These are all examples of accommodations commonly written in a student's IEP. Why not just integrate the commonly used strategies into the overall design of the lesson? Today's student requires increased flexibility, autonomy, and choice. Supports should not detract from the objective, allow the use of the support, and provide remedial instruction in areas of concern. For example, if the objective is *adding fractions with unlike denominators*, the computations will require an understanding of multiplication. If a student struggles with multiplication, allow them to use a calculator because it doesn't detract from the main objective.

To determine what accommodations can support class-wide engagement and overall diversity, leaders should partner with educators holding expertise on learner variability to better understand what accommodations support concept attainment for various learner types. Notice my language; I did not say "partner with special educators" or "partner with individuals familiar with accommodations and modifications." This was on purpose. I have seen leaders blindly assume that special education teachers and leaders have expertise in these areas when, typically, they are generalists and have not been trained to deeply understand what accommodations specifically support concept attainment for literacy or math.

Review the list of commonly used accommodations in Table 6.6 and highlight those that you might consider integrating into your school-wide instructional systems.

Effective Inclusive Reading Instruction

Did you know that students with disabilities and other at-risk learners do not receive sufficient reading instruction or reading intervention (Gilmour et al., 2019)? Do you know if the special education teachers in your school understand the elements of effective reading instruction or whether general education teachers understand the elements of effective reading instruction for exceptional learners? In my first few years as a special education teacher, not only did my preparation program not include content on effective reading instruction, but not even one of my principals coached me on reading instruction nor came into my classroom to observe. An in-depth exploration of the elements of effective reading instruction is beyond the scope of this book, but it is essential to a holistic instructional program designed to improve outcomes for exceptional learners.

The cornerstone of an effective reading program for all students is a comprehensive evidence-based approach to teaching reading. Structured literacy is such an approach. It emphasizes teaching foundational skills explicitly and systematically. This approach supports all learners, but specifically students with

TABLE 6.6 Common Class-Wide Accommodations

Presentation	Response	Setting	Timing	Organization Skills
◆ Provide audio of text ◆ Provide content in alternative formats (video, audio, text) ◆ Reduce the amount of text ◆ Larger text size ◆ Text read aloud ◆ Provide oral and/or written instructions ◆ Recorded notes versus written notes ◆ Provide written notes or lesson outline	◆ Provide options for responding (e.g., written, verbal) ◆ Provide a scribe for dictation ◆ Record responses on audio recorder ◆ Dictionary or spellchecker ◆ Use calculator or fact charts for math	◆ Offer a preferred location or choice for completing assignments ◆ Preferred or strategic seating ◆ Provide specialized lighting or acoustic options ◆ Small-group or individual testing ◆ Provide sensory tools and supports	◆ Extended time ◆ Additional processing time ◆ Strategic and/or frequent breaks (work for 15 minutes or complete set number of problems) ◆ Allow multiple sessions for completing assessments ◆ Allow preferred timing for completing assessment	◆ Use timers ◆ Use highlighter to mark up texts ◆ Use a planner ◆ Teach study skills

dyslexia and other reading problems. Essential characteristics include the following:

- **Explicit Instruction.** Clear direct teaching of reading skills.
- **Systematic.** Logically sequenced instruction with skills building upon one another.
- **Multisensory.** Instructional methods integrate auditory, visual, kinesthetic, and tactile approaches.
- **Focus on Language Structure.** Lessons teach the structure of the English language to include a focus on sounds, patterns, word parts, syntax, and semantics (Ray, 2020).

Effective reading instructional blocks should include structures such as

- lesson design that incorporates the principles of universal design,
- explicit instruction,
- targeted practice and feedback,
- strategic use of staff during the reading block,
- balance of whole-group and small-group instruction,
- targeted differentiation through small groups, and
- increased small-group, teacher-directed instruction for students below grade-level.

Effective Inclusive Math Instruction

Let's start with the obvious, any student who struggles in math should receive math instruction from someone who understands math content standards. Many students with disabilities are supported by general and special education teachers who lack sufficient content expertise (Griffin et al., 2022). Specifically, they don't understand the learning characteristics of students with math difficulties, effective teaching approaches for these students, and effective progress monitoring. Leaders must create systems to strengthen teacher expertise in this area and provide targeted coaching for teachers of students with specific math learning needs.

Effective inclusive math instruction should include the following:

- High-quality math curriculum
- Systematic and explicit instruction that includes pre-teaching new concepts, skills and vocabulary, modeling concepts and computation skills, using multiple examples, connecting to prior knowledge, and using think alouds
- Physical and pictorial representations
- Opportunities for students to demonstrate understanding through representations
- Explicit instruction on how to discuss and justify thinking
- Immediate feedback and error correction
- Vocabulary instruction across core and intervention programs
- Cognitive strategy instruction (Fuchs & Fuchs, 2001; Krawec et al., 2013; Griffin et al., 2022).

Intensity Pulse Check

IMPORTANT: If you don't answer and strategize around the response to the following questions, math outcomes for your exceptional learners WILL NOT improve. Complete the *Intensity Pulse Check* reflection to answer the following:

- *Is your current approach to <u>reading and math</u> sufficiently intensive to promote growth for exceptional learners? What gaps exist between your approach and the core practices outlined in this section?*

Core Practice 3: Personalized Learning Structures

Description: Flexible academic structures that cater to the individual needs of students through differentiated instruction, flexible pacing, and alternative pathways or various routes for students to engage in learning based on their readiness, learning profiles, and needs.

Every student doesn't need the same type or amount of instruction. Inclusive schools design academic blocks that are tiered, flexible, support differentiation, and grounded in high-quality instruction. A student-centered instructional approach must be supported by flexible learning pathways and a structure that allows teachers to attend to students who need varying tiers of support—this is also known as personalized learning. The average classroom includes students who are ready to access the general education curriculum, while others can only make progress through a small-group instructional model. The reality is exceptional learners require, and all students benefit from, targeted instruction and differentiation, which can only be made possible through flexible instructional blocks.

Consider our three learner profiles, Shawn, Isaiah, and Darryl. The teacher is beginning a lesson on the Pythagorean theorem. Mastery of this topic will require advanced problem-solving skills, processing ability, and working memory, to name a few. Shawn, Isaiah, and Darryl represent a snapshot of the students sitting in the average classroom. Personalized learning is essential to their success and essential to supporting the learner variability that exists in your schools. The essential characteristics of personalized learning include the following:

- ◆ **Flexible pacing** – Learners do not process information or master concepts at the same rate. The traditional structures of academic blocks are a mismatch with this scientifically supported concept. Allow students to progress through lessons at their own pace, but with parameters; we can't give students an infinite amount of time, but the premise is that students process information at different rates and may need more time to master certain concepts than others.
- ◆ **Integrate student voice** – Giving students the opportunity to make choices in assignment selection, pacing, or learning modality will support their autonomy, increasing their motivation and engagement.
- ◆ **Alternative pathways** – Alternative pathways allow students to engage in a differentiated set of learning activities based on their readiness, learning profile, and personalized learning plans. Instead of starting the whole class

with the same whole-group mini-lesson, teachers can use a structure inspired by the principles of blended learning or the Modern Classroom where each student starts in a different place based upon their individual learning profile. Flexible structures allow teachers to attend to students who may need pre-teaching while others with accelerated readiness begin independently exploring new content on their own through videos, readings, or other modalities.

Learner Profiles

Shawn

Isaiah

Darryl

- Resilient and motivated learner
- Has dyslexia (struggles with spelling and reading fluency)
- Experiences low mood, anger, and defensiveness
- Thrives in a positive and supportive environment

- Strong long-term memory and motivated to learn
- Requires structure, routines, and positive reinforcement
- Has Autism (uneven cognitive skills, stimming, and repetitive behaviors)
- Lagging skills in emotional regulation (managing frustration)

- Highly motivated, independent worker who grasps complex concepts well
- Proficient in reading, math, and science
- Has ADD (fidgets and seeks touch stimulation)
- Resilient and collaborative learner

FIGURE 2.1 Learner Profiles for Tailored Instruction. This figure presents profiles of three diverse learners—Shawn, Isaiah, and Darryl—highlighting their strengths, challenges, and specific needs.

> *Reflect*: Take a moment and think about how you would ideally design a 60 minute math block that supports Darryl, Shawn, and Isaiah. Jot down your ideas in the space below.

Let's go back to our learner profiles. Considering the same lesson on the Pythagorean theorem, each student may start the lesson at a different point. Isaiah may need to begin with a remedial lesson on equations, Shawn and Darryl begin by exploring key terminology and formulas together, while others start in a mini-lesson with the teacher (see Figure 6.4). By creating alternate pathways, educators can attend to these learners' needs

Lesson Goal: Understand the Pythagorean Theorem as a way to calculate distance and apply it to real-world problems.

	Darryl Shawn	Advanced Multilingual Learners	Gifted and Talented Learners	Isaiah and similar learners
Task 1	• Watch online animated video about Pythagorean Theorem			
Task 2	• Partner to review vocabulary • Watch online direct instruction video	• Complete online tutoring session on square roots and equations	• Online direct instruction video	• 1:1 mini-lesson breaking down formula and key vocabulary
Task 3	• Guided practice with teacher	• Watch online direct instruction video	• Guided practice with small groups	• Review key vocabulary and formulas with a partner
Task 4	• Online practice videos	• Guided practice with teacher	• Check-in with teacher	• Small group direct instruction with special educator
Task 5	• Independent practice and assessment	• Independent practice and assessment	• Independent practice and assessment	• Independent practice and assessment with paraprofessional support

Alternative Pathways: Same Objective, Different Journey

FIGURE 6.4 Differentiated Approaches to the Pythagorean Theorem. This figure illustrates how diverse learners, including advanced multilingual and gifted students, can achieve the same learning objectives through varied instructional pathways.

while working, ensuring they are working toward the same objectives. Ultimately, all students access the same mini-lesson, practice activities, and assessment. A great example of this concept is the Modern Classroom, a structure designed around the principles of personalized learning. You can find useful resources for various grade levels and content areas on their website www.modernclassrooms.org.

What About Differentiation?

Differentiated instruction is often discussed, yet in my experience, it is seldom practiced in schools. One reason this might be true is that the design of the instructional block and curricular choices don't support its use. Differentiated instruction can support all learners but is often reserved for subgroups. I like to think of differentiation as creating a pathway to learning based on who students are as individual learners. Teachers should meet the range of learners in their classrooms.

Differentiated instruction is defined as the use of targeted strategies based on an individual student's needs. The alternative pathway example in Figure 6.5 is a great illustration that

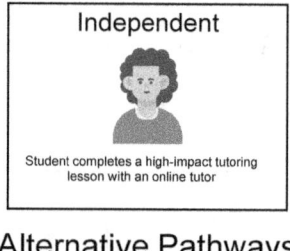
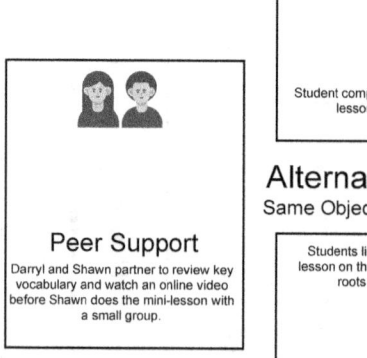

FIGURE 6.5 Differentiated Pathways to Achieve a Shared Objective. This figure illustrates various instructional approaches—including peer support, independent work, remedial lessons, and small group collaboration—that enable diverse learners to meet the same academic goal through tailored strategies.

can help leaders distinguish between universally designing a lesson and removing barriers to learning for all students and differentiation.

Universally Designed
- Animated video to introduce lesson: Provide information in multiple modalities to promote access
- Creation of multiple pathways to objective mastery
- Provide multiple assessment options

Differentiation
- Isaiah's 1:1 mini-lesson focuses on vocabulary and concept breakdown (other student's mini-lesson won't be as bite-sized).
- Small-group direct instruction will vary for Isaiah (simpler problems) and gifted students (complex equations and multistep problems).
- Isaiah's assessment will include simpler problems and be scaffolded to have him explain how to break down every step of the process to support his information processing and see where his understanding lies.

It is important to note that there may be some overlap between strategies used to make the overall lesson accessible and differentiation for targeted students. The goal is to do both with intentionality.

Core Practice 4: Targeted Interventions

Description: Intensive (higher frequency and duration) individualized skill remediation that supplements, rather than replaces, grade-level instruction, using evidence-based strategies such as one-on-one tutoring and small-group instruction.

Intervention isn't intervention unless it's intensive, iterative, and expertly designed—anything less is just good intentions masquerading as support. So, what are you supposed to do? Commit to increasing the intensity of interventions that are strategically focused, tightly monitored, and adapted with surgical precision—because intensity isn't optional; it's the difference between progress and failure (Lemons et al., 2018). Students with disabilities need a more intensive approach to their instructional support if they are ever to make appropriate progress (Fuchs et al., 2018). Students unresponsive to Tiers 1 and 2 face two unfortunate outcomes: they either remain stuck in Tier 2 with ineffective interventions or move to special education, only to be placed back in the general classroom that failed to meet their needs initially (Fuchs & Fuchs, 2017). The solution is more intensive interventions coupled with the other core practices in this section.

Effective interventions should be based on the area of need but also connected to grade-level instructional goals. They must be tiered, supplemental, and evidence-based. There are no shortcuts here. Table 6.7 should be integrated into your instructional planning protocols and inform the design of your intervention programming. It describes the key characteristics of Tier 1, Tier 2, and Tier 3 interventions.

A common pitfall in intervention-service delivery is replacing grade-level instruction with intervention. Intervention blocks *should not* replace grade-level instruction and must reinforce standards-based goals that are aligned with the grade-level curriculum. Many students with more extensive needs will require long-term interventions.

TABLE 6.7 Targeted Intervention Protocol

Element	Tier 2	Tier 3
Frequency	30 minutes/day, 4 times per week	60 minutes/day 5 times per week
Duration	8–10 weeks	
Format	Homogenous small groups	1:1
Content	Research-based interventions Systematic and explicit instruction	Research-based interventions Systematic and explicit instruction
Progress Monitoring	Targeted rate of improvement must be set Progress monitored weekly	Targeted rate of improvement must be set Progress monitored weekly

Source: Griffin et al. (2022).

In math, effective interventions should be (1) individualized, (2) intensive, and (3) inclusive of strategies designed to promote the transfer of learning (Fuchs & Fuchs, 2001). The latter is often missing in the way schools approach intervention. Transfer of learning requires explicit instruction on how to apply skills learned in intervention sessions to the regular classroom context.

For students with math deficits, effective intervention includes the following:

- **Diagnose.** Identify and target student needs
- **Validated Intervention.** Implement proven methods
- **Explicit, Systematic Instruction.** Provide targeted and structured teaching
- **Personalized.** One-on-one or small group
- **Active Participation.** High rates of prompting and responding
- **Scaffolding and De-scaffolding.** Provide cues and prompts then reduce them over time
- **Effective Feedback.** Give specific and actionable feedback
- **Respond to Data.** Adjust instruction based on ongoing assessments (Carnine, 1997; Woodward & Montague, 2002; Fuchs et al., 2018; Lemons et al., 2018)

Intensity Pulse Check

IMPORTANT: If you don't answer and strategize around the response to the following questions, math outcomes for your exceptional learners WILL NOT improve. Complete the *Intensity Pulse Check* reflection to answer the following question:

- ✓ Is your current approach to <u>intervention</u> sufficiently intensive to promote growth for exceptional learners?

Core Practice 5: High-Quality Specialized Instruction

Description: Effective, evidence-based instructional strategies tailored to meet the unique needs of students with disabilities. Targeted supports should ensure instruction is both effective and aligned with IDEA mandates.

Specialized instruction, or specially designed instruction (SDI) refers to adapting the content, methodology, or delivery of instruction to address the unique needs of a student with a disability, as defined by the Individuals with Disabilities Education Act (IDEA, 2004). SDI aims to ensure these students can access the general education curriculum and meet the educational standards applicable to all students. SDI should be tailored to the individual student's needs and be outlined in the student's IEP.

There are three critical elements of SDI: content adaptation, methodology adaptation, and delivery of instruction. Despite its critical importance, SDI alone is often insufficient to improve outcomes for students with disabilities (Fuchs et al., 2018). Many special educators do not have content expertise in literacy or math, yet they are responsible for delivering the SDI required for students with literacy or math goals. Many other factors contribute to the ineffectiveness of SDI, such as a lack of coaching and feedback from coaches with expertise in the content area and an expert understanding of SDI, excessive caseloads resulting in limitations on instructional effectiveness, and poorly designed roles that spread educators too thin.

To effectively implement SDI, teachers need structured, consistent, and regularly scheduled co-planning periods, limits on the number of grade levels they serve, and ongoing professional development. Leaders can also work with their districts to identify strategies for reimagining roles and responsibilities to ensure students receive targeted support from the most qualified individuals. Leaders should also ensure teachers utilize effective and targeted instructional strategies for students with more extensive support needs, such as response prompting, peer support strategies, embedded instruction, and self-determination strategies.

Chapter Summary

Effective implementation of student-centered instructional systems depends on a collaboration between the school leader, who must create a supportive schedule and allocate necessary resources, and the teacher, who then organizes students within the provided structures. Student-Centered Instruction empowers teachers to attend to the varying needs in a classroom, and it must become the new standard operating procedure in school. Bringing these core practices to life requires a strategic improvement process that includes the following:

- Creating a vision for inclusive instructional systems
- Selecting a high-quality curriculum
- Strategically hiring and assigning staff to support a student-centered model that drives improved outcomes
- Creating a schedule that supports quality instruction, personalization, intervention, and collaboration
- Building staff capacity to support instructional effectiveness (see Chapter 7 for details on what staff should know)
- Monitoring and coaching teachers on core content and intervention instruction
- Effectively managing change

Your Role

The call to action for leaders is to:
Disrupt general education so all kids can learn.

Meeting the academic needs of exceptional learners will require a commitment to reimagining instructional policies, practices, and protocols. All stakeholders must play a role in intensifying our response to the chronically low performance of exceptional learners. Principal managers, district leaders, and policymakers must transform the conditions necessary for school-based leaders to transform and redesign existing academic systems while other vital partners play a contributing role.

What role can you play? Use Table 6.8 to identify how you can partner in answering the call to action for *Student-Centered Instruction*.

In the next chapter, you will examine the systems, practices, and protocols necessary to drive strong instructional decision-making: *data*.

TABLE 6.8 Stakeholder Roles in Student-Centered Instruction

Stakeholder Role	Disrupt General Education So All Kids Can Learn
School Leader (Principal, Executive Director, Assistant Principal, etc.)	Create flexible instructional systems that normalize a personalized approach to tiered instruction grounded in rigorous grade-level content that is universally designed to meet the needs of exceptional learners.
Principal Managers and District Leaders	Offer leaders flexibility in systems design and providing appropriate resources to support inclusive instructional systems.
	Interrupt siloes between curriculum and instruction and specialized programs (e.g., special education, bilingual education) to permit collaboration and integration of inclusive education principles in practices into a districtwide approach to teaching.
Funders	Ensure funding priorities intentionally include exceptional learners by requiring grantee initiatives to deliberately mitigate or remove barriers to promote success for exceptional learners.
School Support Organizations	Ensure academic initiatives support schools with improving outcomes for exceptional learners.
Policymakers	Mandate academic initiatives (e.g., MTSS; UDL) that improve outcomes for exceptional learners and creating policies or incentives that require schools to intentionally mitigate or remove barriers to promote success for exceptional learners.
Families and Caregivers	Educate yourself about effective reading and math strategies aligned to your child's individual needs. Ask for guidance in providing at-home support to strengthen your child's academic growth.

Your Equity Skills

In Chapter 1, I introduced you to the *Five Abilities of Equity Literacy* (Gorski & Swalwell, 2023), which are the five skills leaders should possess to become true equity leaders. In the last chapter, you reflected on those skills in the context of discipline and behavior as you considered how you would transform those systems to disrupt inequity and actively cultivate equity in your schools.

Let's now apply those same tenets to your school's approach to instruction and reflect on whether your systems promote or prevent equity for exceptional learners. We'll start by reviewing the five skills in relation to Student-Centered Instruction; you'll then reflect on each in your context.

Recognize Inequity. In what ways might your instructional policies, practices, or protocols be inequitable or negatively affecting exceptional learners? This chapter outlined the core practices essential to driving growth for exceptional learners: Tiered Instruction, Universally Designed Instruction, Personalized Learning Structures, Targeted Interventions, and High-Quality Specialized Instruction. Your system is inequitable if existing policies, practices, or protocols conflict with those practices' characteristics.

Review Table 6.9 to reflect on your equity abilities within your instructional systems. When you finish, you will be ready to review the *call to action* and set your individual goals in the final section of this chapter, "Action Planning."

TABLE 6.9 Equity Abilities: Student-Centered Instruction

Equity Abilities	*Reflection Question*	*Potential Response*
Recognize Inequity *Identify how policies, practices, or protocols are negatively affecting exceptional learners*	♦ Do my academic policies and practices disadvantage students with academic challenges or disabilities? ♦ Is there a mismatch between the design of our academic schedule, course offerings, or staffing structures and the academic needs of exceptional learners?	♦ Classrooms prioritize whole-group instruction ♦ General educators do not consider learner variability in lesson design ♦ Students with math disabilities receive intervention from teachers without math expertise ♦ Schedule does not allow for grade-level instruction and remediation
Respond to Inequity *Address the impact of the inequitable practice (e.g., educate, repair harm)*	♦ What steps can I take to change policies and protocols so they no longer disadvantage students with academic needs or disabilities?	♦ Revise the academic block to allow for small-group instruction ♦ Integrate special education teachers into academic blocks ♦ Assign special educators to one content area and build their content expertise ♦ Rewrite unit plans to integrate principles of UDL

(Continued)

TABLE 6.9 (CONTINUED) Equity Abilities: Student-Centered Instruction

Equity Abilities	Reflection Question	Potential Response
Redress Inequity *Identify the root cause of the inequity and eliminate it*	◆ What organizational norms or traditions led to the inequitable policy? ◆ What underlying beliefs or mindsets led to the inequitable policies?	◆ Teacher roles are siloed ◆ Expertise is siloed ◆ Schedule was not developed in collaboration with inclusive education or special education experts
Cultivate Equity *Develop and/or revise policies, protocols, practices, and procedures that promote justice for exceptional learners*	◆ What routines can be embedded into our academic blocks or planning protocols to support exceptional learners proactively? ◆ What common accommodations should be integrated into our classroom and school-wide systems?	◆ Revamp professional learning and staffing protocols to promote strategic integration of expertise on inclusive education
Sustain Equity *Create support structures and accountability systems to maintain equity*	◆ What are the enabling conditions necessary to maintain instructional systems that are empowering to exceptional learners and sustainable for teachers?	◆ Crosswalk all written policies and protocols to ensure alignment with the new policy ◆ Integrate step-back meetings to reflect on policy implementation into pre-existing data analysis protocols

From Knowing to Doing: Driving Change for Student-Centered Instruction

None of the information in this chapter is newly discovered. Yet, even among schools considered inclusive, most are not implementing effective inclusive practices (Copeland & Cosbey, 2009; Rojewski et al., 2013; Hehir et al., 2016; Taylor et al., 2020; McLeskey et al., 2022b). We can no longer simply focus on school improvement and reform; prioritizing incremental improvements and improving academic outcomes for exceptional learners will require us to intensify our approach to instruction and commit to redesigning our academic systems to integrate inclusive practices. Schools must strategically align personnel, create a robust schedule integrating grade-level instruction and intervention, leverage evidence-based instructional materials, maximize time use, and strategically leverage educators. The principal must lead these efforts.

It is not enough to know the elements of effective Student-Centered Instruction. Leaders must also understand that "the best ideas require careful planning and collective action to change classroom and school practices" (Fullan, 2016). Zaretta Hammond introduced me to "seductive shortcuts" (DuFour et al., 2016), which warns against quick fixes without addressing underlying issues.

To go from *knowing* to *doing*, you must consider your action steps in concert with change management principles. ***Skipping the steps outlined in this section will be the difference between success and failure.*** Table 6.10 summarizes those considerations (Tyack & Cuban, 1995; Heath & Heath, 2010; DuFour et al., 2016; Fullan, 2016). It will help guide your planning for designing student-centered instructional systems.

TABLE 6.10 Change Management Considerations: Student-Centered Instruction

Key Steps	Understand and Consider Your Context	Leader Actions
Lay the Foundation	*Identify Your Current State*	♦ Assess current instructional systems to examine what policies, practices, and protocols are promoting inequity. Identify gaps between existing practices and core practices of Student-Centered Instruction.
	Build Relationships and Trust	♦ Gather feedback from community members (teachers, caregivers, students, community members) and engage them in the evaluation process.
	Engage Your Community	♦ Evaluate whether you have the necessary relationships to engage and empower members of your team, staff, and community to drive change in this area.

(Continued)

TABLE 6.10 (CONTINUED) Change Management Considerations: Student-Centered Instruction

Key Steps	Understand and Consider Your Context	Leader Actions
Empower Key Stakeholders	Build Capacity	♦ Provide ongoing professional development and coaching systems to support implementation of instruction at all levels. Strategically assign coaches who can provide targeted feedback aligned to rigorous goals for exceptional learners.
	Create a Compelling Vision	♦ Develop and communicate a vision that prioritizes academic achievement for exceptional learners and realigned expectations and systems.
	Create Systems of Support	♦ Be willing to make courageous decisions when there is misalignment.
	Be Driven by Action	♦ Be empathetic and intentional about addressing the concerns of those affected by the change. ♦ Provide necessary resources to support their ability to navigate the change.
Focus on Outcomes	Use Data to Drive Decision-Making	♦ Set clear goals and create an action plan for each of the core practices aligned to your target area. Δ
	Align Policies and Practices	♦ Develop leading and lagging indicators to help monitor success and inform needed adjustments. Δ
Transform Systems	Ongoing Inquiry	♦ Align policies and practices to allow for an intensified focus on instruction. Relevant policies and practices may include hiring, staffing, scheduling, usage of resources, and design of the school environment. Δ ♦ Eliminate policies and practices that are perpetuating inequity.
Continuous Improvement	Celebrate Success	♦ Create a system for ongoing inquiry to improve practices. Δ ♦ Evaluate whether redesign or new policies and practices are creating or perpetuating inequity. ♦ Determine whether exceptional learners are making progress and benefiting from the new system. ♦ Be flexible and responsive to feedback. Δ
	Understand and Consider Your Context	♦ Celebrate wins, milestones, and achievements to motivate staff and build momentum. Δ

> **TRANSFORMING YOUR INSTRUCTIONAL SYSTEMS**
>
> **Reflect:** *What change management considerations are going to be key for your context?*

Action Planning

The following is an expanded version of the table you saw at the beginning of this chapter. The nuance distinguishing typical practices from disruptive status-quo-breaking action lies in the details. Review the shifts in the last column and answer the questions that follow. You'll then use this reflection and your understanding of *Student-Centered Instruction* to identify your next steps and begin action planning.

TABLE 6.11 The Three Problems and Solutions: Student-Centered Instruction

Problem	Potential Solutions
The Ownership Problem *Are the correct individuals accountable for this challenge?*	♦ Strategic coaching for special educators ♦ Provide targeted professional development in literacy and math for special educators ♦ Develop clear accountability structures that define roles and expectations ♦ Ensure administrators support and monitor the collaboration between general and special educators
The Design Problem *Does the design of the learning environment promote belonging and social-emotional well-being for exceptional learners?*	♦ Redesign learning environments to promote success for exceptional learners ♦ Schedule flexible blocks that allow for both grade-level and remedial instruction
The Knowledge Problem *Do all educators understand effective practice in this area?*	♦ Provide ongoing professional development focused on effective inclusive practices and learner variability ♦ Build content expertise in special educators ♦ Hire reading and math specialists into a special education role ♦ Train teachers and leaders on HLP in special education

> *Reflect:*
>
> ♦ Which shifts seem most likely to improve outcomes for your exceptional learners?

Planning Template

Planning Task	Notes
Final Reflection Are the correct individuals accountable for this challenge?	
Goal Craft one goal aligned with the content of this chapter.	
Resources What resources are needed to meet this goal? Consider human capital, scheduling, and finances.	

Bibliography

American Speech-Language-Hearing Association. (n.d.). Disorders of reading and writing. ASHA. https://www.asha.org/practice-portal/clinical-topics/written-language-disorders/disorders-of-reading-and-writing/

Barringer, M.D., Pohlman, C., & Robinson, M. (2010). *Schools for all kinds of minds: Boosting student success by embracing learning variation.* Jossey-Bass.

Billingsley, B., DeMatthews, D., Raab, R.R., & James, L. (2022). Principal actions in effective inclusive schools: a review of elementary case studies. In J. McLeskey, N. L. Waldron, F. Spooner, & B. Algozzine (Eds.), *Handbook of effective inclusive elementary schools* (2nd ed., pp. 16–42). Routledge.

Carnine, D. (1997). Instructional design for students with learning disabilities. *Journal of Learning Disabilities*, 30(2), 130. https://doi.org.hoover2.mcdaniel.edu:2443/10.1177/002221949703000201

CAST. (2024). Universal Design for Learning guidelines version 3.0. http://udlguidelines.cast.org

Connor, D. (2014). Social justice in education for students with disabilities. In *The SAGE Handbook of Special Education: Two Volume Set* (2nd ed., Vol. 2, pp. 111–128). SAGE Publications Ltd, https://doi.org/10.4135/9781446282236

Copeland, S. R., & Cosbey, J. (2009). Effective instructional practices to support the inclusion of students with extensive support needs in general education classrooms. *Research and Practice for Persons with Severe Disabilities*, 33(4), 214–227.

Courtade, G., Jimenez, B., Root, J., & Pennington, R. (2022). Planning for effective inclusive instruction in core content. In J. McLeskey, N. L. Waldron, F. Spooner, & B. Algozzine (Eds.), *Handbook of effective inclusive elementary schools* (2nd ed., pp. 286–301). Routledge.

Danielson, C. (2007). *Enhancing professional practice: A framework for teaching* (2nd ed.). Association for Supervision and Curriculum Development.

Darling-Hammond, L. (2010). *The flat world and education: How America's commitment to equity will determine our future*. Teachers College Press.

Department of Education, Office of Special Education and Rehabilitative Services. (2015, November 16). Dear Colleague Letter on Free Appropriate Public Education (FAPE).

DuFour, R., DuFour, R., Eaker, R., Many, T., & Mattos, M. (2016). *Learning by doing: A handbook for professional learning communities at work* (3rd ed.). Solution Tree Press.

Endrew, F. V. Douglas County School District RE-1, 580 U.S. (2017).

Fritzgerald, A. (2020). *Antiracism and Universal Design for Learning: Building expressways to success*. CAST, Inc.

Fuchs, D., Fuchs, L. S., McMaster, K. L., & Lemons, C. J. (2018). Students with disabilities' abysmal school performance: An introduction to the Special Issue. *Learning Disabilities Research & Practice*, 33(3), 127–130. https://doi.org/10.1111/ldrp.12180

Fuchs, L. S., & Fuchs, D. (2001). Principles for the Prevention and Intervention of Mathematics Difficulties. *Learning Disabilities: Research & Practice*, 16(2), 85–95.

Fuchs, L. S., & Fuchs, D. (2017). Intervention and Referral Services: Response to Intervention. In S. R. Jimerson, M. K. Burns, & A. M. VanDerHeyden (Eds.), *Handbook of Response to Intervention: The Science and Practice of Multi-Tiered Systems of Support* (2nd ed., pp. 61–75). Springer.

Fullan, M. (2016). *Coherence: The right drivers in action for schools, districts, and systems*. Corwin Press.

Gilmour, A. F., Fuchs, D., & Wehby, J. H. (2019). Are Students With Disabilities Accessing the Curriculum? A Meta-Analysis of the Reading Achievement Gap Between Students With and Without Disabilities. *Exceptional Children*, 85(3), 329–346. https://doi.org/10.1177/0014402918795830

Gorski, P., & Swalwell, K. (2023). *Fix injustice, not kids and other principles for transformative equity leadership*. ASCD.

Grant, A. (2023). *Hidden potential: The science of achieving greater things*. Viking.

Griffin, C., Kwon, J. B., Apraiz, K., & Wong, L. N. (2022). Creating opportunities for struggling mathematics learners in inclusive schools. In J. McLeskey, N. L. Waldron, F. Spooner, & B. Algozzine (Eds.), *Handbook of effective inclusive elementary schools* (2nd ed., pp. 221–244). Routledge.

Hammond, Z. (2015). *Culturally Responsive Teaching and The Brain: Promoting Authentic Engagement and Rigor Among Culturally and Linguistically Diverse Students*. Corwin.

Heath, C., & Heath, D. (2010). *Switch: How to change things when change is hard*. Crown Business.

Hehir, T., Pascucci, S., Grindal, T., Freeman, B., Lamoreau, R., Borquaye, Y., & Burke, S. (2016). *A Summary of the Evidence on Inclusive Education*. Abt Associates.

Individuals with Disabilities Education Act (IDEA), 20 U.S.C. § 1400 (2004).

International Dyslexia Association. (n.d.). Understanding dysgraphia. Retrieved July 22, 2024, from https://dyslexiaida.org/understanding-dysgraphia/

IRIS Center. (n.d.). What role does fidelity of implementation play in RTI? Vanderbilt University. https://iris.peabody.vanderbilt.edu/module/rti05/cresource/q1/p03/#content

Krawec, J., Huang, J., Montague, M., Kressler, B., & de Alba, A. M. (2013). The Effects of Cognitive Strategy Instruction on Knowledge of Math Problem-Solving Processes of Middle School Students With Learning Disabilities. *Learning Disability Quarterly*, 36(2), 80–92.

Lemons, C. J., Vaughn, S., Wexler, J., Kearns, D. M., & Sinclair, A. C. (2018). Envisioning an Improved Continuum of Special Education Services for Students with Learning Disabilities: Considering Intervention Intensity. In Grantee Submission.

Levenson, N. (2011). Something Has Got to Change: Rethinking Special Education. Future of American Education Project. https://files.eric.ed.gov/fulltext/ED521782.pdf

Marzano, R. J. (2003). Classroom instruction that works: Research-based strategies for increasing student achievement. Association for Supervision and Curriculum Development.

McLeskey, J., Maheady, L., Billingsley, B., Brownell, M. T., & Lewis, T. J. (2022a). *High leverage practices for inclusive classrooms* (2nd ed.). Routledge.

McLeskey, J., Waldron, N. L., Spooner, F., & Algozzine, B. (2022b). Time to support inclusion and inclusive schools. In J. McLeskey, N. L. Waldron, F. Spooner, & B. Algozzine (Eds.), *Handbook of effective inclusive elementary schools* (2nd ed., pp. 3–13). Routledge.

Novak, K. (2016). *UDL now! A teacher's guide to applying Universal Design for Learning in today's classrooms* (2nd ed.). CAST Professional Publishing.

Novak, K. (2022). *In support of students: A leader's guide to equitable MTSS*. Corwin.

Ray, J. S. (2020). Structured Literacy Supports All Learners: Students At-Risk of Literacy Acquisition - Dyslexia and English Learners. *Texas Association for Literacy Education Yearbook*, 7, 37–43.

Rojewski, J. W., Lee, I. H., & Gregg, N. (2013). Causal effects of inclusion on postsecondary education outcomes of individuals with high-incidence disabilities. *Journal of Disability Policy Studies*, 25(4), 210–219. https://doi.org/10.1177/1044207313505648

Sayeski, K. L., Bateman, D. F., & Yell, M. L. (2019). Re-Envisioning Teacher Preparation in an Era of "Endrew F.": Instruction over Access. *Intervention in School and Clinic*, 54(5), 264–271. https://doi.org.hoover2.mcdaniel.edu:2443/10.1177/1053451218819157

Taylor, J. P., Rooney-Kron, M., Whittenburg, H. N., Thoma, C. A., Avellone, L., & Seward, H. (2020). Inclusion of students with intellectual and developmental disabilities and postsecondary outcomes: A systematic literature review. *Inclusion*, 8(4), 303–319. https://doi.org/10.1352/2326-6988-8.4.303

Tyack, D., & Cuban, L. (1995). *Tinkering toward utopia: A century of public school reform*. Harvard University Press.

U.S. Department of Education. (n.d.). Sec. 300.116 Placements. Individuals with Disabilities Education Act. Retrieved July 4, 2024, from https://sites.ed.gov/idea/regs/b/b/300.116

Understood. (n.d.-a). What is a specific mathematics disability? Understood.org. https://www.understood.org/en/articles/what-is-a-specific-mathematics-disability

Understood. (n.d.-b). What is dyslexia? Understood.org. https://www.understood.org/en/articles/what-is-dyslexia

Woods, A.D. Glosky, C., Wang, Y., & Morgan, P. (2023). A Multivariate Meta-Analysis of the Effects of Business-as-Usual Special Education Services in U.S. Schools. https://doi.org/10.31234/osf.io/fs3zg).

Woodward, J., & Montague, M. (2002). Meeting the challenge of mathematics reform for students with LD. *The Journal of Special Education*, 36(2), 89–101.

Principle 5

Data Urgency

The call to action for leaders is to:
Urgently collect and use data.

Old Thinking: We wait until we have data showing students are struggling before intervening.
New Thinking: We plan ahead for potential struggles and intervene immediately.

In This Section

We can't sit around and wait for students to fail before we act. Moving beyond the status quo for exceptional learners requires increased urgency around how educators collect and use data to maximize student performance. Educators collect rich sets of data every day and should leverage that data to make immediate decisions to drive improved student performance. In this section, leaders will explore strategies for using short (e.g., daily, weekly) and long-term data cycles to drive instructional decision-making. The call to action to leaders is to:

Urgently collect and use data.

> **CHAPTER CONTENTS**
>
> ♦ Be Urgent About Data
> ♦ The Rapid Response Protocol: Real-Time and Short-Term Data Cycles
> ♦ The Truth About Progress Monitoring
> ♦ Long-Term Data Cycles

Be Urgent About Data

As we saw in the introduction to this book, all school-wide systems should be grounded in a systematic approach to supporting students. Strategic systems for collecting, analyzing, and responding to data are at the heart of that approach. MTSS, a multitiered system of supports, should be the framework leaders use to drive their approach to building a data-savvy culture. Data collection through the MTSS framework is straightforward:

- **Screen All Students**. Administer a universal screener to all students to identify who is on track for grade-level performance and who needs additional support.
- **Identify Students for Support**. Use guidelines provided by the assessment tool to identify students in need of additional support.
- **Develop and Implement Support Plan**. Develop a plan that outlines supports to be integrated into general education instruction, strategic interventions, and intensive interventions.
- **Monitor Progress**. Conduct formal progress monitoring on a weekly or biweekly basis to monitor improvement toward grade-level performance using a norm-referenced assessment (an assessment that compares students to their peers).
- **Observe Instruction**. Monitor skill attainment during intervention delivery.
- **Adjust**. Adjust interventions accordingly.

In my work with leaders, steps four and five are the most underutilized. Often, progress monitoring is not frequent enough, or educators only evaluate skill attainment on individual interventions and don't use a norm-referenced assessment tool to track progress toward generalized reading and math. In addition to a robust formal assessment system, leaders must create consistent structures for responding to daily and weekly classroom performance. What is the point of teaching if we don't know whether our students are mastering the skills taught? This is a critical reason why we aren't seeing substantive progress for exceptional learners in school. When I was a teacher, the only time my student data was analyzed was when IEP progress reports were due, and that was every nine weeks. That means for nine weeks, students were struggling, and no immediate action was taken to identify why they were struggling and to create targeted support plans. We can't wait for, nor rely on, formal assessments (interim, standardized, screeners) to make instructional changes in support of exceptional learners. The next section outlines specific strategies to increase urgency in how you respond to data.

The Rapid Response Protocol: Real-Time and Short-Term Data Cycles

Leaders need a structured and systematic data analysis process that empowers teachers to strategically plan responsive instruction for students who do not meet expectations. The high-leverage practices for inclusive classrooms instruct educators to use assessment information to analyze and adjust instruction as needed and to provide positive and constructive feedback to students (McLeskey et al., 2022). The Rapid Response Protocol prioritizes five key actions to support strong data analysis and response:

- **Plan for Misconceptions**: During instructional planning, identify potential misconceptions for all students and those that might present for specific student learning profiles.
- **Plan for Feedback**: Identify which students will need strategic monitoring during instruction and create a plan to monitor individual student responses.

- **Monitor and Provide Feedback**: Provide immediate and corrective feedback based on student responses.
- **Short-Term Data Meeting**: Review student performance on formative and summative assessments (e.g., quizzes, tests) to identify students who need targeted support.
- **Implement Support Plan**: Create and implement targeted support plans and monitor progress.
- **Repeat**.

This protocol evolved from the approach I originally developed for the leadership institute I founded, where I coached hundreds of leaders. It draws on established data protocols 1 and research 2 to drive increased equity for exceptional learners and has been further developed through collaboration with other practitioners.

Plan for Misconceptions

During instructional planning, educators should collaborate to determine the priority standards, essential learnings, and potential misconceptions. Educators need to plan scaffolds in response to how potential misconceptions may impact objective mastery for the critical mass of students and the misconceptions that may present because of a student's specific learning profile. In my work with leaders, I have seen them substantively engage in the first task (identify potential misconceptions for the critical mass of students) but miss that critical next step of considering individual learning profiles. Consider our three student learner profiles (see Figure 7.1) and the following task (Table 7.1):

RAPID RESPONSE PROTOCOL

Plan for Misconceptions	Plan for Feedback	Monitor and Provide Feedback	Short-Term Data Meeting	Implement Support Plan
During instructional planning, identify potential misconceptions and those that might present for specific student learning profiles	Identify to strategically monitor during instruction and create a plan to monitor individual student responses	Provide immediate and corrective feedback based upon student responses	Review student performance on summative assessments (e.g. quizzes, tests) to identify students in need of targeted support	Create and implement targeted support plan, monitor progress

FIGURE 7.1 Rapid Response Protocol for Addressing Misconceptions. This figure outlines a structured approach for identifying, monitoring, and addressing student misconceptions through strategic planning, targeted feedback, and data-driven interventions to ensure timely and effective support.

TABLE 7.1 Standard and Task

Standard	Analyze how a modern work of fiction draws on themes, patterns of events, or character types from myths, traditional stories, or religious works such as the Bible, including describing how the material is rendered new. (Common Core State Standards, ELA-Literacy.RL.8.9)
Task	Write an essay comparing a theme from a classic myth to a theme in a contemporary novel. Use specific examples from both texts to support your analysis.

One potential misconception that many students may have is misinterpreting the plot as a theme. While Shawn may also have this misconception, her dyslexia may also cause her to struggle with fully extracting and comprehending the theme of each text. Recognizing this potential misconception in advance will support Shawn's teachers with planning appropriate scaffolds and effectively preparing for providing feedback.

Learner Profiles

Shawn

- Resilient and motivated learner
- Has dyslexia (struggles with spelling and reading fluency)
- Experiences low mood, anger, and defensiveness
- Thrives in a positive and supportive environment

Isaiah

- Strong long-term memory and motivated to learn
- Requires structure, routines, and positive reinforcement
- Has Autism (uneven cognitive skills, stimming, and repetitive behaviors)
- Lagging skills in emotional regulation (managing frustration)

Darryl

- Highly motivated, independent worker who grasps complex concepts well
- Proficient in reading, math, and science
- Has ADD (fidgets and seeks touch stimulation)
- Resilient and collaborative learner

FIGURE 2.1 Learner Profiles for Tailored Instruction. This figure presents profiles of three diverse learners—Shawn, Isaiah, and Darryl—highlighting their strengths, challenges, and specific needs.

Plan for Feedback

The next step is to identify which students will need strategic monitoring during instruction and create a plan to monitor their performance. Knowing that confusing plot with theme is a likely misconception, teachers can script out specific checks for understanding aligned to that potential error to support all learners. The teacher should include in her plan which students she will target for immediate feedback and during what point of the lesson to help maximize their work time. For example, once she completes the lesson and students are released for independent practice, she may want to check in with Isaiah first to support him in getting started, given his low frustration tolerance. Armed with the knowledge that Shawn will likely struggle with extracting and comprehending the themes of the text, the teacher should also pre-plan feedback that she will provide to Shawn if that error presents. She may direct her to write out the theme for each text and then check in with Shawn again to review her responses and provide feedback before she begins her comparative analysis. This degree of targeted planning increases the likelihood of student success on a given task.

Reflect: *Have you seen this level of intentionality in planning feedback to support exceptional learners? What are the implications?*

Daily Feedback Rounds

Once teachers have answered the questions of who to check in with, when, and how often, they are ready for the next step: monitoring for specific errors during guided and independent practice and providing immediate and corrective feedback. Again, the absence of this level of intentionality can result in wasted time, lack of mastery, and students falling further behind. Feedback must be intentional and high quality, as follows:

- **Goal-Directed**: Aligned to the goals of the lesson.
- **Specific**: Provides clear instructions on what to do next.
- **Constructive**: Lets students know what steps are needed to improve.
- **Immediate**: Monitors students while they are working and provides feedback at critical stages.
- **Respectful and Positive**: Focuses on progress, not deficits.
- **Communicates High Standards**: Conveys that mistakes are due to high expectations, not low capability.

♦ **Reassuring**: Communicates to students that they can improve with effort (McLeskey et al., 2022; Hammond et al., 2014).

If students aren't responsive to feedback, teachers should plan interventions or small-group instruction. I have seen leaders develop a variety of approaches for daily data analysis. There is no perfect approach—the overarching goal is to answer, *"Are students learning? If not, what can we do about it?"*

Collecting and reviewing data daily may seem like overkill, but it doesn't have to be complicated. In our daily lives, we regularly gather and use data to make decisions about what we do and when. Knowing that schools are struggling with driving sufficient growth for exceptional learners, they must be vigilant about determining whether provided supports are working, where learning gaps exist, and creating a plan to respond. Here are some examples of how I have seen leaders collect and use data daily (Figure 7.2).

Here are some questions leaders can consider as a part of a daily data review protocol to increase Data Urgency and immediate action planning:

♦ Was there any unfinished work or assessments? Will this impact mastery of priority standards?
♦ Who did not master the day's exit ticket?

Same Day Coaching	Immediate Remediation	Data-Based Small Groups
• Track and post exit ticket assessment average for each period. • When leaders see low performance trends they check-in with individual teachers to problem solve and create a coaching plan or plan to adjust the lesson or instruction.	• Special education leaders monitor exit ticket mastery for their students. • Leaders check in with teachers to problem solve and identify misconceptions • Leaders and teachers develop an immediate plan for remediation	• During instructional period, co-teachers monitor guided and independent practice and identify students who need additional instruction and use that data to create same day small groups • Teacher with the strongest content knowledge leads remedial small groups for the lowest performers

FIGURE 7.2 Data-Driven Instructional Planning and Monitoring. This figure illustrates the cyclical process of using student data to plan, implement, and monitor instructional strategies. It highlights key stages, including identifying misconceptions, providing targeted feedback, and adjusting instruction based on assessment outcomes to ensure effective student learning outcomes.

- Was there any unexpected student performance?
- Were there barriers within the lesson or environment that led to incomplete work or lack of mastery?
- Will there be sufficient practice opportunities over the course of the week to increase mastery?
- What adjustments are needed to upcoming lessons, interventions, or assessments?

Review and reflect: *What systems and structures need to be in place to support this level of daily data analysis? What is the potential impact on students?*

Inclusive Short-Term Data Meeting

Leaders can leverage short-term data meetings to support Data Urgency. These meetings are structured opportunities to review student performance on classroom assessments to identify students needing targeted support. For this process, preparation is key. Leaders facilitating and educators participating in these meetings must clearly understand what students were expected to learn, how they should have demonstrated that learning, and what common misconceptions might have led to student errors. Making this process equity-centered asks leaders to ensure the protocol integrates a discussion of how an individual student's learning profile might have impacted their performance and whether there were barriers present during instruction that impacted their mastery. Success in this process requires the participation of both general education and special educators to analyze student performance collaboratively.

Key questions that should be included in this data analysis protocol can be found in Table 7.2.

Reflect: *Which question do you think can have the greatest impact on the performance of exceptional learners? Why?*

The frequency of short-term data meetings can vary depending on your context, but they should be frequent enough to ensure students are making meaningful progress. In *Driven by Data*, Paul Bambrick-Santoyo recommends *weekly* data analysis to support immediate student support planning (2010). This frequency is suggested for analyzing overall student performance, reinforcing

TABLE 7.2 Short-Term Data Protocol: Key Questions and Strategies for Analyzing Data to Address Student Needs Effectively

Key Data Review Questions	Essential Considerations for Exceptional Learners
What were students expected to master in general education by the end of the week?	Were exceptional learners working toward rigorous goals? Did students receive high-quality accessible instruction? (see checklist in Chapter 3)
Did students receive accessible instruction?	Were there barriers presented within the classroom environment or instructional design that prevented students from accessing or demonstrating understanding of the content?
What were this week's intervention goals?	Did students receive quality intervention?
What were the potential misconceptions?	Did teachers plan appropriate scaffolds to mitigate misconceptions?
What were the performance and error trends?	How might learner variability have led to additional errors?
What support approach will close student gaps? Do students need a targeted reteach aligned to the misconception, small-group interventions, explicit instruction, practice on remedial skills, or something else?	If there is a barrier in the original design of instruction (e.g., accessibility), how will that be remediated? What can be remediated within general education? Who needs targeted interventions? More intensive interventions? How will we align specialized instruction?
What teacher gaps need to be addressed (e.g., quality of planning or instruction, ability to respond to data)?	How will we ensure teachers understand how to select and plan appropriate scaffolds, interventions, and supports for exceptional learners?

the argument that improving outcomes for exceptional learners requires increased urgency. If it is recommended to conduct *weekly* data meetings to analyze data for *all students*, our approach to data analysis for exceptional learners must be more urgent.

Implement Support Plan

Once educators have created a support plan, the plan should be implemented with fidelity and monitored. Each structured meeting should include a plan for follow-up to support implementation and an ongoing cycle of analysis and response (2010). A system for predictable and recurring data analysis and response is critical to improving outcomes for exceptional learners (National

Center for Education Evaluation et al., 2009). The Rapid Response Protocol is designed to answer, "Do we have a plan to maximize student learning? Are students learning? If not, what will we do about it?" If we don't know how our exceptional learners perform daily or weekly, then we won't move beyond the status quo.

Leaders should use the What Works Clearinghouse (ies.ed.gov/ncee/wwc) or the National Center for Intensive Intervention (intensiveintervention.org) to identify research-informed or evidence-based interventions. Interventions for exceptional learners should not be haphazardly selected or implemented. They should be tailored using a research-based approach for determining intensity, such as *The Taxonomy for Intervention Intensity* (see Table 7.3) as outlined by go-to experts in tiered intervention delivery, Lynn and Douglas Fuchs (2017).

TABLE 7.3 Intervention Intensity: Key Dimensions and Guiding Questions for Implementing Effective Interventions

Intensity Dimension	*Questions for Leaders to Consider*
Strength	How effective is the program for students needing intensive interventions as indicated by effect sizes?
Dosage	How frequently do students have opportunities to respond and receive corrective feedback?
Alignment	Does the program address all of the student's academic skill deficits, avoid covering already mastered skills, and focus on grade-appropriate standards?
Attention to Transfer	Does the intervention help students apply learned skills to different contexts and connect mastered skills to related ones?
Comprehensiveness	Does the intervention include explicit instruction principles such as clear explanations, strategy modeling, ensuring background knowledge, gradual support reduction, ample practice opportunities, and systematic review?
Behavioral Support	Does the program include components for self-regulation, executive function, and behavioral principles to minimize nonproductive behavior?
Individualization	Is there a validated, data-based process in place for special educators to adjust interventions over time to meet the complex needs of students?

The Truth About Progress Monitoring

In addition to responding to assessment during and after instruction, leaders must create a system for formal progress monitoring using measures that evaluate the impact of instruction and intervention on student growth targets (Filderman & Toste 2018). Students receiving intensive intervention should have growth goals aligned with grade-level targets. The goals should be formally progress monitored using curriculum-based tools that are reliable, meaningful, efficient; can be repeatedly administered; are sensitive to improvement; and are linked to external accountability measures (2014a). Two examples of such tools are Dibels and AIMSWeb. Dibels is a literacy assessment tool for grades kindergarten through eighth grade that monitors the development of key literacy skills. AIMSWeb is an example of an assessment tool that monitors the development of key literacy and math skills for grades kindergarten through 12 (University of Oregon, n.d.).

Formal progress monitoring determines whether interventions result in grade-level performance improvement. Simply assessing skills being taught during intervention is not enough. Progress monitoring frequency should align with the intensity of the intervention. Table 7.4 outlines the recommended frequency of progress monitoring as outlined by the CEEDAR Center, a national technical assistance center for schools. To ensure the sustainability and feasibility of this process, leaders should consider how to integrate an analysis of progress monitoring data

TABLE 7.4 Progress Monitoring Frequency: Recommended Data Collection Schedules for Different Intervention Tiers

Intervention Tier	Frequency of Progress Monitoring
All Students (Tier 1)	Three times per year (fall, winter, spring)
Students Receiving Targeted Interventions (Tier 2)	Every two to four weeks
Students with Disabilities and Students Receiving Intensive Interventions (Tier 3)	Weekly or biweekly

Source: Bailey et al. (2020).

into existing collaboration systems or into their system for short-term data analysis.

Long-Term Data Cycles

For at least the past 20 years, schools have become increasingly adept at implementing formalized assessment cycles and leveraging them to support planning. Schools typically administer screening assessments at multiple points throughout the school year to identify student grade-level performance and students in need of targeted intervention. Examples of universal screeners (two of these may sound familiar from our progress monitoring discussion!) are Dibels, AIMSWeb, and NWEA MAP. Schools also administer interim assessments on a recurring cycle (typically quarterly) to evaluate student progress on grade-level standards and curriculum. These assessments are a part of a long-term data cycle of assessment and planning. Long-term data cycles are used to develop targeted goals, identify students in need of additional support, and identify students for further diagnostic assessment. Those goals and supports should be evaluated as a part of a school's progress monitoring systems.

An in-depth discussion of long-term data cycles is beyond the scope of this book, but these considerations will help leaders create effective data and assessment systems for exceptional learners.

- **Ground Data Planning in MTSS**: Data planning meetings should be grounded in MTSS's tiered structure.
- **Use Validated and Reliable Screening Tools**: Select tools that have strong evidence of accuracy, reliability, and validity.
- **Administer and Score Assessments with Fidelity**: Ensure assessment administration follows set guidelines and administrators receive proper training.
- **Analyze and Use Screening Data Effectively**: Define how data will be used before analysis. Use data to evaluate core programs and identify intervention needs.

♦ **Include Strengths and Weaknesses in Discussions**: Data meetings should include discussions of learners' strengths and weaknesses. Leverage language from the neurodevelopmental framework (introduced in Principle 2, from Barringer et al.).

By grounding data planning in MTSS, using reliable tools, maintaining fidelity in administration, and effectively analyzing data, schools can strengthen instructional decision-making and better meet the needs of exceptional learners.

Your Equity Skills

Let's return to our equity skills. We reflected on these skills in the context of the other two school-wide systems: instruction and culture. Let's do our final reflection on data. Again, we must practice using these skills if we are going to be adept at driving equity in our schools (2023).

Now that you've spent some time understanding the principle of *Data Urgency*, you are ready to reflect on whether the data systems in your school are promoting or preventing equity for your exceptional learners. Review Table 7.5 and answer the reflection questions to reflect on your context.

TABLE 7.5 Equity Skills: Data Urgency: Reflection Questions and Responses for Addressing Equity Through Data Use

Equity Abilities	Reflection Question	Potential Response
Recognize Inequity Identify how policies, practices, or protocols are negatively impacting exceptional learners	♦ Do my data review protocols practices disadvantage exceptional learners? ♦ Do they advantage one subgroup over another? ♦ Are assessment tools or targets based on one group's norms or traditions to the detriment of other groups? What are the implications of this?	♦ During interim assessment cycles, we create reteach plans for students on the bubble. By design, this disadvantages students with disabilities who are significantly below grade level. This creates an opportunity gap and perpetuates the performance gap for this subgroup.

(Continued)

TABLE 7.5 (CONTINUED) Equity Skills: Data Urgency: Reflection Questions and Responses for Addressing Equity Through Data Use

Equity Abilities	Reflection Question	Potential Response
Respond to Inequity *Reactive Response* Address the impact of the inequitable practice (e.g., educate, repair harm)	◆ What adjustments to the policy are necessary to remove disadvantages to exceptional learners?	◆ Revise policy and align appropriate resources to ensure students with the most significant needs have access to supports needed to close the performance gap.
Redress Inequity *Proactive Response* Identify the root cause of the inequity and eliminate it	◆ What organizational norms or traditions led to the inequitable policy? ◆ What underlying beliefs or mindsets led to the inequitable policies?	◆ Our accountability system puts pressure on us to increase the overall percentage of students meeting proficiency targets. It is easier to meet these targets by focusing on students who are closer to proficiency. ◆ Underlying beliefs may include "students with certain disabilities will never meet proficiency targets, so we won't prioritize them."
Cultivate Equity Develop and/or revise policies, protocols, practices, and procedures that promote justice for exceptional learners	◆ What routines can be embedded into our daily schedule that allow us to more strategically respond to the data of exceptional learners? ◆ What schedule changes are necessary to ensure that exceptional learners have excess to the increased levels of support needed to support their growth?	◆ Create a schedule that provides special educators time to review daily and weekly data performance for exceptional learners. ◆ Create a flexible block within the student schedule to allow additional time for remediation.
Sustain Equity Create support structures and accountability systems to maintain equity	◆ What are the enabling conditions necessary to maintain data analysis systems that are empowering to exceptional learners and sustainable for teachers?	◆ Crosswalk all written policies and protocols to ensure alignment with the new policy. ◆ Integrate stepback meetings to reflect on policy implementation into pre-existing data analysis protocols.

Chapter Summary

This chapter emphasizes the critical need for urgency in using data to inform instruction for exceptional learners. Equity-driven leaders intentionally transform data systems to disrupt the status quo to drive positive academic outcomes for these students.

Effective data analysis must include planning for potential misconceptions, monitoring instructional effectiveness, and determining when to intervene. Educators should leverage both short-term (daily, weekly) and long-term data cycles to drive instructional decisions. The Rapid Response Protocol serves as a key strategy that prioritizes planning for misconceptions, feedback delivery, instructional monitoring, short-term data meetings, and implementing support plans.

Additionally, progress monitoring and long-term data cycles are essential for evaluating the impact of interventions and ensuring continuous student growth. Leaders must create systems to support this robust data response process and can make it more feasible by integrating systems into existing collaboration structures.

The chapter calls for a shift in systems design, a change in perspective regarding accountability, and a shared commitment to reimagining equity. Without a sense of urgency, the needs of exceptional learners will continue to go unmet, and they will fall further behind.

Your Role

The call to action for leaders is to:
Urgently collect and use data.

Review Table 7.6 to identify your role in supporting Data Urgency in schools. Answer the reflection question that follows.

TABLE 7.6 Stakeholder Roles: Roles of Educators, Leaders, and Families in Supporting Data-Driven Equity Efforts

Stakeholder Role	I Can Support Data Urgency
School Leader (Principal, Executive Director, Assistant Principal, etc.)	Create protocols for urgent data analysis. Create an aligned schedule to support teachers in this process. Build teacher capacity in the Rapid Response Protocol.
Principal Managers and District Leaders	Provide tools to support robust data collection and analysis. Provide tools to support efficiency.
Funders	Integrate accountability for growth of exceptional learners into grant requirements.
School Support Organizations	Build internal capacity on understanding how to leverage data to support. exceptional learners, integrate data analysis for exceptional learners into school support strategy.
Policymakers	Create or improve accountability requirements for improved academic outcomes for all subgroups. Create incentives for schools to improve outcomes for exceptional learners. Revise incentive programs that overlook the performance of subgroups, ensuring that the growth of exceptional learners is always a contingency for recognition or rewards.
Families and Caregivers	Request an outline for each unit and corresponding assessments, ask teachers to provide weekly/biweekly reports on classroom and intervention performance with specific feedback and suggested interventions.

Planning Template

Planning Task	Notes
Final Reflection *Are your data practices sufficiently urgent to improve outcomes for exceptional learners?*	
Goal *Craft one goal aligned with the content of this chapter.*	
Resources *What resources are needed to meet this goal? Consider human capital, scheduling, and finances.*	

Bibliography

Bailey, T. R., Colpo, A. & Foley, A. (2020). Assessment Practices Within a Multitiered System of Supports (Document No. IC-18). Retrieved from University of Florida, Collaboration for Effective Educator, Development, Accountability, and Reform Center website: http://ceedar.education.ufl.edu/tools/innovationconfigurations/

Bambrick-Santoyo, P. (2010). *Driven by data: A practical guide to improve instruction*. John Wiley & Sons.

Filderman, M. J., & Toste, J. R. (2018). Decisions, Decisions, Decisions: Using Data to Make Instructional Decisions for Struggling Readers. *TEACHING Exceptional Children*, 50(3), 130–140. https://doi.org.hoover2.mcdaniel.edu:2443/10.1177/0040059917740701

Fuchs, L. S., Fuchs, D., & Malone, A. S. (2017). The taxonomy of intervention intensity. *Teaching Exceptional Children*, 50, 35–43. doi: 10.1177/0040059917703962

Hammond, Z. Jackson, Y., Alpert, D. Greenberg, K. Schroller, A. Hill, K. (Eds), Culturally Responsive Teaching & The Brain (1st Ed.), *Citing excerpts from Establishing Alliance in the Learning Partnership*. Corwin: California. (2014). (pp. 104–105).

McLeskey, J., Maheady, L., Billingsley, B., Brownell, M. T., & Lewis, T. J. (2022). *High leverage practices for inclusive classrooms* (2nd ed.). Routledge.

National Center for Education Evaluation and Regional Assistance (ED), What Works Clearinghouse (ED), Hamilton, L., Halverson, R., Jackson, S. S., Mandinach, E., Supovitz, J. A., & Wayman, J. C. (2009). Using Student Achievement Data to Support Instructional Decision Making. IES Practice Guide. NCEE 2009-4067. National Center for Education Evaluation and Regional Assistance.

University of Oregon. (n.d.). About DIBELS. Dynamic Measurement Group. https://dibels.uoregon.edu/about-dibels

Part 3
Putting It All Together

8

Principle 6

Collective Responsibility

Commit to Being a Part of the Solution, No Matter Your Role

"The distance between knowledge and action can be measured in courage."

— Author Unknown

Now that you know what to do, are you willing to do it? We can no longer sit around and wait for someone else to do the work. Each of us must make a commitment *today* to play a part in making school work for every single student, especially exceptional learners. I am no longer satisfied with hoping, trying to convince, or waiting for others to decide that exceptional learners matter and doing what it takes to create schools where they can thrive. Getting there will require individuals like you and me to seek positions of power, seek public office, break out of siloed special education roles, and take on general education roles. If you ask yourself, "Can I improve the system in my current role?" and the answer is no, the question becomes, "Am I okay with this? If not, what do I need to do?"

There are several leaders and organizations who have courageously stepped outside of the box, making substantive commitments to supporting exceptional learners in their work.

- ♦ Bob Runcie, the CEO of Chiefs for Change, has committed to reimagining its core programming to ensure that all chief-level leaders have access to learning experiences that focus on inclusive education.
- ♦ Sonia Park, the executive director of the Diverse Charter Schools Coalition, has become an active partner of the Center for Learner Equity. She actively lobbies for federal and philanthropic funding to increase the center's capacity to integrate special education initiatives into its work.
- ♦ The philanthropic trio, including Charter School Growth Fund, EdForward DC, and the Camden Education Fund, have collectively made multimillion-dollar funding commitments to support leaders designing inclusive school environments or leading initiatives focused on substantively improving outcomes for students with disabilities. Darryl Cobb, Bisi Oyedele, and Jonathan Garr are the equity-centered leaders at the helm of these efforts.
- ♦ Naomi Shelton, CEO of the National Charter Collaborative, is a fierce advocate for equity and inclusion and an active partner of organizations such as the Center for Learner Equity, a national leader in special education advocacy efforts.
- ♦ Jenny Tan is the chief of schools at KIPP Northern California and made strategic commitments to better supporting students with disabilities. She has elevated a former special education director to founding school leader, invested significant dollars into strengthening the academic program for students with disabilities, and spent significant time building her own knowledge about effective inclusive practice.

One of the many reasons the status quo for exceptional learners persists is that not enough people are taking responsibility for solving this challenge. We can begin to meaningfully chip away at the chronically poor outcomes for these students once we collectively commit to change. Typically, it's the special educator waiving the red flag of concern as it relates to advocating for a commitment to inclusivity, stronger academic systems, and supportive behavior systems. However, these individuals typically don't have the locus of control necessary to drive change. That power rests in the hands of those in positions of power: superintendents, principals, funders, boards, and school authorizers. It is those individuals who own the responsibility of change.

Know Your Role in Supporting Inclusive Equity

Helping to achieve equity for exceptional learners is everyone's duty. There isn't a single individual in our society who will not be involved in or directly impacted by the education system. This system creates the citizens who live within and run our communities. Given the weight of this responsibility, it is crucial for every individual to recognize and comprehend their role in ensuring the effective support of all learners within our education system, particularly those who have been or are likely to be marginalized—our exceptional learners.

While principals are considered the central catalysts for creating and sustaining effective, inclusive school environments, others can support their efforts.

I have penned personal letters to each stakeholder type hoping to elicit your commitment today.

My Letter to You

Dear Principals,

As a school leader, you see every day how the environment can make or break a student's experience. Imagine your school where every student—regardless of their differences—feels they belong, participates fully, and are genuinely prepared for life beyond graduation. You have the power to make this a reality. By embracing the mindset that "every kid is my kid," you can create a culture where inclusive practices are not just hopes and dreams. Who is the student who needs your commitment today?

Dear Superintendents and District Leaders,
You didn't go into district leadership because you love policy-making—you likely sought to lead change and drive achievement. Your leadership sets the tone that is felt in every classroom in your district. Picture a district where every school shares a commitment to inclusivity, teachers are equipped to meet the needs of all learners, and where disciplinary practices empower rather than exclude. Your decisions determine who becomes what when they leave school. Please make a commitment today!

Dear Philanthropists,
You profoundly impact the academic experience of students who need the most from school by the decisions you make every day. Who gets support, and who does not? Imagine the ripple effect of a simple decision to prioritize initiatives that remove barriers for kids who have often been left out. By prioritizing programs that promote inclusivity, you're not just funding projects—you're opening doors to a brighter future for every child. How can you ensure that your funding efforts promote success for the students who need you the most?

Dear Families and Caregivers,
I understand the joy of seeing your child thrive in a classroom where they are truly seen, valued, and supported. I also know the pain of hearing a teacher tell you that your child doesn't fit in. Your voice and involvement matter so much. How can you strengthen your commitment to your child and other learners so that your child feels accepted, succeeds in school, and helps others do the same, like the kids at Chas's school?

Dear School Support Partners,
You are the innovators, the cheerleaders, and the support system. Without you, schools would struggle to meet the complex needs of their students. You do so much to support schools every day. How can you take your commitment a step further by working to ensure your efforts meaningfully touch every learner, especially those who need the most from school? What commitment can you make today to broaden your impact and be a true changemaker?

Review the responsibilities aligned to your role and make one commitment to being a part of the solution (Table 8.1).

TABLE 8.1 Summary of Stakeholder Roles Across Principles

Stakeholder Role	Design for Marginalized Learners	Support Inclusive Professional Learning	Reframe Discipline Systems as Social-Emotional Support Systems	Disrupt General Education So All Kids Can Learn
School Leader (Principal, Executive Director, Assistant Principal, etc.)	Ground academic, behavioral, and discipline policies, procedures, and protocols in inclusive values and set expectations aligned to those values.	Embed continuous professional learning opportunities into existing structures, focusing on learner variability and inclusive practices.	Ground discipline policies, procedures, and protocols in inclusive values and set expectations aligned to those values. Build staff capacity to understand behavior science and effective behavior support. Create coaching systems to provide feedback to educators.	Create flexible instructional systems that normalize a personalized approach to tiered instruction grounded in rigorous grade-level content that is universally designed to meet the needs of exceptional learners.
Principal Managers and District Leaders	Set a vision for inclusivity, align district-wide expectations to an inclusive vision, and allocate resources to support that vision.	Set a vision for inclusivity, align district-wide expectations to this vision, and allocate resources for professional development on learner variability.	Set district-wide expectations around proactive and positive approaches to behavior. Allocate resources to support that vision.	Offer leaders flexibility in systems design and provide appropriate resources to support inclusive instructional systems. Interrupt silos between curriculum and instruction and specialized programs (e.g., special education, bilingual education) to permit collaboration and integration of inclusive education principles into a district-wide approach to teaching.

(Continued)

TABLE 8.1 (CONTINUED) Summary of Stakeholder Roles Across Principles

Stakeholder Role	Design for Marginalized Learners	Support Inclusive Professional Learning	Reframe Discipline Systems as Social-Emotional Support Systems	Disrupt General Education So All Kids Can Learn
Funders	Ensure funding priorities intentionally include exceptional learners by requiring grantee initiatives to deliberately mitigate or remove barriers to promote success for exceptional learners.	Prioritize funding for professional development initiatives that include training on learner variability and inclusive teaching practices.	Develop funding priorities and requirements focused on positive, proactive, and supportive behavior and discipline practices.	Ensure funding priorities intentionally include exceptional learners by requiring grantee initiatives to deliberately mitigate or remove barriers to promote success for exceptional learners.
School Support Organizations	Ensure all programming and initiatives support schools in improving outcomes for exceptional learners.	Design all programs and initiatives to include components that train and support educators in understanding and addressing learner variability.	Ensure that programming provided to schools regarding behavior, discipline, and mental health includes a focus on effectively supporting exceptional learners.	Ensure academic initiatives support schools in improving outcomes for exceptional learners.

Policymakers	Mandate practices that improve outcomes for exceptional learners and create policies or incentives that require schools to intentionally mitigate or remove barriers to promote success for exceptional learners.	Mandate professional development practices that include training on learner variability and create policies or incentives that promote inclusive education for exceptional learners.	Mandate practices, create policies, or offer incentives requiring schools to prioritize a proactive, positive, and supportive approach to behavior.	Mandate academic initiatives (e.g., MTSS, UDL) that improve outcomes for exceptional learners and create policies or incentives that require schools to intentionally mitigate or remove barriers to promote success for exceptional learners.
Families and Caregivers		Educate yourself about learner variability and model and encourage inclusive attitudes and behaviors.	Educate yourself about proactive and positive behavior strategies. Collaborate with your child's school to develop strategies to strengthen your student's social, behavioral, or emotional skills.	Educate yourself about effective reading and math strategies aligned to your child's individual needs. Ask for guidance in providing at-home support to strengthen your child's academic growth.

Note: The first row for Families and Caregivers continues: "Educate yourself about learner variability and participate in school-based training or workshops to model and encourage inclusive attitudes and behaviors."

Summary of Stakeholder Roles Across Principles

Write your commitment below and then go to the book's website (www.thetonibarton.com) to share your commitment. Our kids need you!
    Your Commitment:

Closing

As we close the chapter on our learning journey, let us remember Michael, Thasya, Darryl, and Isaiah—real students who sat in classrooms across this country, yearning for an education that nurtured their hopes and dreams. Let their stories be a reminder that every student has the right and the ability to thrive when provided the right support. We have a duty to create schools where every single student feels welcome and empowered, leaving the schoolhouse doors filled with potential and opportunity.

The Problem

Back Matter

> This book starts where most conversations about disability justice in schools—or, really, any form of justice in schools—never quite seem to arrive. We're urged to think and act institutionally and systemically, not just interpersonally.
> — Paul Gorski

This is not just another book on inclusive education. This book is about justice.

This is not just another book that talks about the problem. This book offers solutions.

This is not just a list of shiny new practices. This is a *call to action* because we know what works, yet inclusivity remains elusive to far too many students, educators, and schools.

A school is only *truly* inclusive if students, regardless of difference or ability, are thriving academically and are experiencing belonging. The reality is that students who need the most from school are being left behind every single day.

Students with disabilities, neurodivergent learners, multilingual learners, and even gifted and talented students, have been consistently underperforming for the entire 20 years that I have been in education. Now, many other students are falling further and further behind.

We CAN fix this, but it will require urgency and a shift in our thinking about school design!

Inclusive education can no longer be an effort focused only on students with disabilities because the current crises being faced by schools—from low attendance to lack of engagement to falling reading scores—require a response focused on shifting the design of school systems, policies, and practices.

If you are tired of the same old rhetoric and believe it's time to do school differently, this book is for you.

Let's explore six principles that can move us from school reform to school transformation as we answer the call from the students who are asking us to do more.

"That, in essence, is what Toni Barton gifted me—gifted all educators—in this book. She shifted the ways I think about and, as a result, the ways I will act on inequity in schools and beyond. Shift a perspective, transform every related practice." —Paul C. Gorski, founder of the Equity Literacy Institute and coauthor (with Katy Swalwell) of *Fix Injustice, Not Kids and Other Principles for Transformative Equity Leadership*

Learn more and access free tools at www.thetonibarton.com.

For Product Safety Concerns and Information please contact our EU
representative GPSR@taylorandfrancis.com
Taylor & Francis Verlag GmbH, Kaufingerstraße 24, 80331 München, Germany

www.ingramcontent.com/pod-product-compliance
Lightning Source LLC
Chambersburg PA
CBHW071017240426
43661CB00073B/2479